The Silk Road

Explore the World's Most Famous Trade Route

WITH 20 PROJECTS

Antioch
Khiva
Bukhara
Samarkland
Kashgar
Turfan
Hami
Merv
Bactria
Dunhau

Kathy Ceceri
Written & Illustrated

green press
INITIATIVE

Nomad Press is committed to preserving ancient forests and natural resources. We elected to print *The Silk Raod: Explore the World's Most Famous Trade Route* on 4,007 lbs. of Williamsburg Recycled 30% offset.

Nomad Press made this paper choice because our printer, Sheridan Books, is a member of Green Press Initiative, a nonprofit program dedicated to supporting authors, publishers, and suppliers in their efforts to reduce their use of fiber obtained from endangered forests. For more information, visit www.greenpressinitiative.org

Nomad Press
A division of Nomad Communications
10 9 8 7 6 5 4 3 2 1

This book was manufactured by Sheridan Books,
Ann Arbor, MI USA.
January 2011, Job #322986
ISBN: 978-1-934670-65-1

Illustrations by Kathy Ceceri

Questions regarding the ordering of this book should be addressed to
Independent Publishers Group
814 N. Franklin St.
Chicago, IL 60610
www.ipgbook.com

Nomad Press
2456 Christian St.
White River Junction, VT 05001
www.nomadpress.net

Contents

Map, Timeline, and People

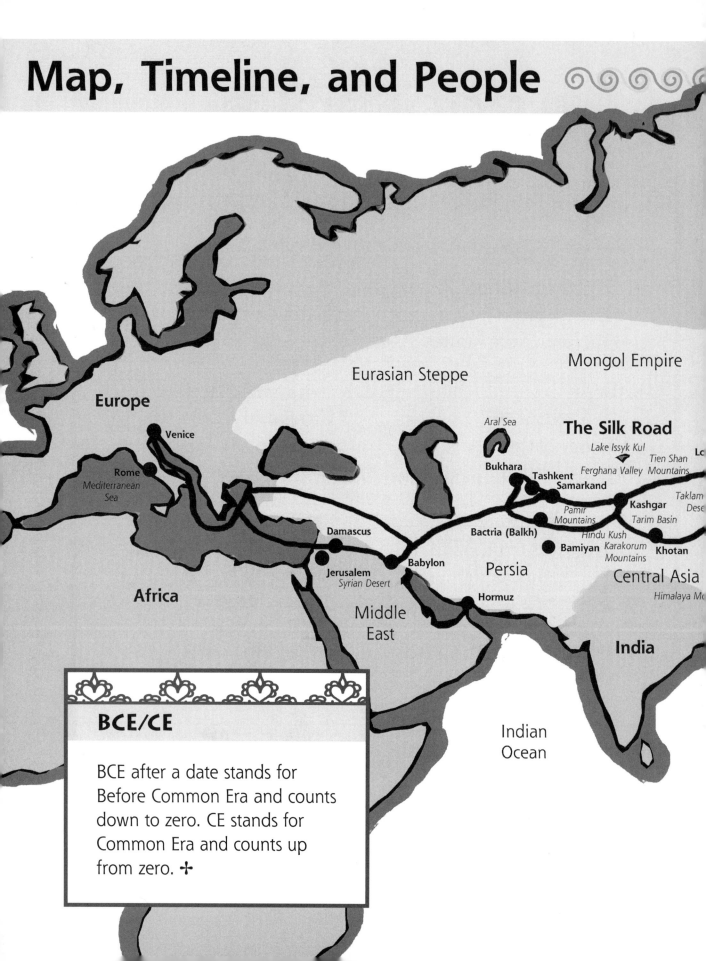

Mongol Empire

Eurasian Steppe

Europe

Aral Sea

The Silk Road

Lake Issyk Kul

Tien Shan Lc
Mountains

Venice

Bukhara

Tashkent

Ferghana Valley

Rome

Samarkand

Taklam

Mediterranean Sea

Pamir Mountains

Kashgar

Dese

Tarim Basin

Bactria (Balkh)

Damascus

Hindu Kush

Babylon

Jerusalem
Syrian Desert

Persia

Bamiyan

Karakorum Mountains

Khotan

Central Asia

Africa

Middle
East

Hormuz

Himalaya Mo

India

BCE/CE

BCE after a date stands for
Before Common Era and counts
down to zero. CE stands for
Common Era and counts up
from zero. ✛

Indian
Ocean

BCE

5000 Chinese begin trade with Central Asia on Jade Road.

2700 Long-distance trade begins along Tin Road.

550–486 King Darius (522–486), ruler of the Persian Empire, builds Persian Royal Road.

330 Alexander the Great (356–323), leader of the Greek Empire, conquers Central Asia.

138 Zhang Qian (?–114), considered the "father of the Silk Road" sets off for Central Asia and Persia.

106 Han Dynasty in China, ruled by Emperor Wudi (156–87), sends first trade caravan along Silk Road to Persia.

CE

14 Roman Empire tries to ban silk robes for men.

70 Kushan Empire encourages Silk Road trade through Central Asia.

65 Buddhist missionaries sent from India to China.

20 Roman, Parthian, Kushan, and Chinese empires begin to collapse, limiting Silk Road trade.

618 Tang Dynasty in China reopens Silk Road

635 Nestorian Christians arrive in China.

1096 Christians begin Crusades against Muslims in the Middle East.

1196 Genghis Khan (1167–1227) creates Mongol Empire.

1260–1368 *Pax Mongolica.*

1264 Kublai Khan (1215–1294) founds Yuan Dynasty in China.

1271–1295 Marco Polo (1254–1324) journeys to China along the Silk Road.

1368 Ming Dynasty pushes Mongols out of China and ends Silk Road trade.

1325 Ibn Battuta (1304–c.1377), a Muslim scholar, begins a long journey along the Silk Road.

1369 Timur (1336–1405) attacks Central Asia to control Silk Road. Tries to revive Mongol Empire.

1453 Muslim rulers in Turkey close Silk Road to Christian Europeans.

1498 Vasco da Gama opens sea route around Africa to Asia.

1877 Ferdinand von Richthofen (1833–1905) coins the name "Silk Road."

1907 Marc Aurel Stein (1862–1943) finds Diamond Sutra in cave in China.

1998 Yo Yo Ma (1955–) establishes the Silk Road Project to promote the study of cultural traditions along the ancient Silk Road trade routes.

2001 Taliban destroys Silk Road–era Buddha statues in Afghanistan.

2009 Silk Road countries join together to seek membership on UNESCO World Heritage list.

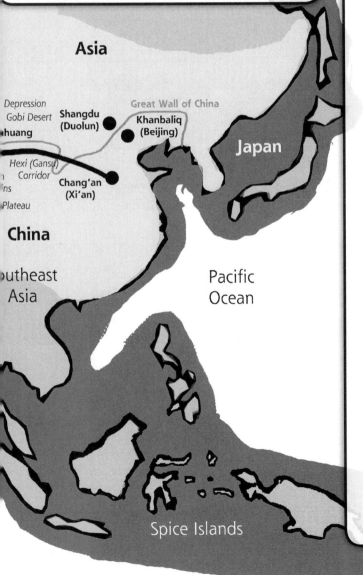

Asia

Depression
Gobi Desert
Shangdu (Duolun)
Khanbaliq (Beijing)
Great Wall of China
huang
Hexi (Gansu) Corridor
Japan
Chang'an (Xi'an)
ns
Plateau

China

utheast Asia

Pacific Ocean

Spice Islands

Other Titles in the *Build It Yourself* Series

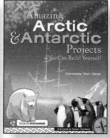

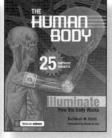

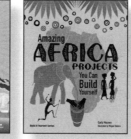

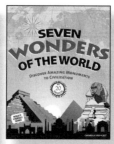
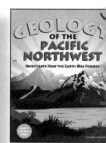

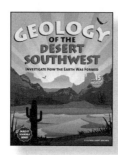

introduction

The Silk Road & Other Ancient Trade Routes

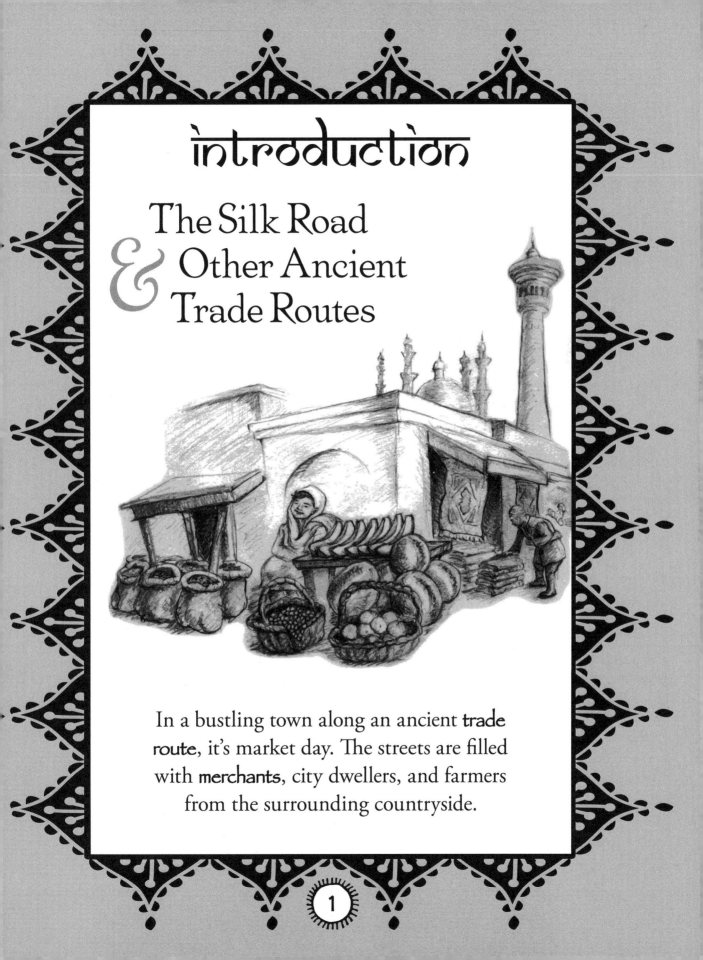

In a bustling town along an ancient **trade route**, it's market day. The streets are filled with **merchants**, city dwellers, and farmers from the surrounding countryside.

Everyone is hoping to make a good sale or a good purchase. Some people drive carts pulled by camels or donkeys. Others arrive on foot.

Rows and rows of booths proudly display every kind of item imaginable. Fabric, jewelry, leather goods, and carpets are laid out for inspection. In one row meat vendors sell sheep, goats, pigs, chickens, and ducks. Down another row neatly stacked piles of melons, grapes, and figs are for sale. An inviting smell comes from a booth filled with sacks of colorful spices—black pepper, yellow sesame seeds, orange **saffron**, red curry powder, and many more.

Bottles of herbal medicine line the shelves of a stall next to some chairs where customers are getting their hair cut or their teeth pulled. Everywhere salespeople call out to passersby. Friends greet each other, traders haggle nose to nose, and children race up and down the alleys in between.

words to know

trade route: a route used mostly to carry goods from one place to be sold in another.

merchant: someone who buys and sells goods for profit.

saffron: a cooking spice.

Silk Road: the ancient network of trade routes connecting the Mediterranean Sea and China by land.

What Is a Trade Route?

Long before the invention of highways, airplanes, telephones, or the Internet, trade routes connected different parts of the world. People used them to carry goods and information across long distances. But these routes weren't like today's roads. Crossing just one section of a trade route could take weeks or months.

Perhaps the most famous trade route of all is the **Silk Road**. The Silk Road was actually a network of east–west paths connecting the Mediterranean Sea and China. It stretched across more than 7,000 miles (11,300 kilometers), or one quarter of the way around the globe.

Fascinating Fact

Before 1877 there was no name for the trade routes between Europe and Asia. That's when a geographer named Ferdinand von Richthofen came up with the term "die Seidenstrasse," German for "the Silk Road."

The Silk Road connected Europe, the Middle East, and Central Asia. Branches of the Silk Road reached to Africa, Japan, China, India, and Southeast Asia. Its main trade good was **silk**, a beautiful, soft fabric from China. But many other **luxury** items were traded back and forth as well. They included glass, carpets, and precious **minerals**.

Trading on the Silk Road began before the **Roman Empire** and lasted until the end of the **Middle Ages**. This trade brought wealth and knowledge to those along the way.

words to know

silk: a delicate and beautiful fabric made from the cocoon of a silkworm.

luxury: something expensive. It is not really needed, but it brings pleasure.

minerals: naturally occurring solids that have a crystal structure. Gold and diamonds are precious minerals. Rocks are made of minerals.

Roman Empire: the nation that ruled much of Europe, Africa, and Asia around the Mediterranean Sea from about 753 BCE to about 476 CE.

empire: a large group of states and people ruled by a king, called an emperor, or a small group of people.

Middle Ages: a period of time from about 350 CE to 1450 CE.

emperor: the ruler of an empire.

missionary: someone who tries to win others to his or her faith.

chapter 1

History of the Silk Road

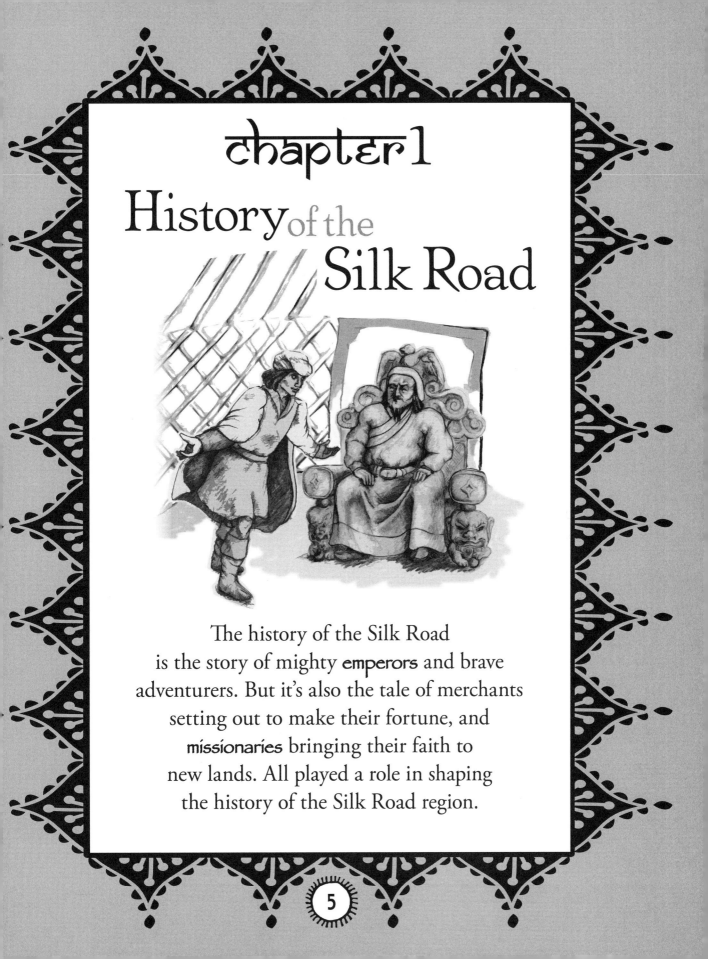

The history of the Silk Road is the story of mighty **emperors** and brave adventurers. But it's also the tale of merchants setting out to make their fortune, and **missionaries** bringing their faith to new lands. All played a role in shaping the history of the Silk Road region.

TRADE AND TRAVEL BEFORE THE SILK ROAD

People began using parts of the Silk Road as far back as 5,000 years ago. At first, short trade routes connected neighboring areas. Then traders on these short routes began to exchange goods with traders from other routes. This created long delivery chains that passed goods back and forth over much greater distances than most merchants were willing to travel. Some early routes that became parts of the Silk Road include:

ᵟ **The Jade Road:** China began importing jade from Central Asia around 5000 BCE. Jade is a hard, shiny stone, found in pale green, cream, brown, and other colors. It was used for carvings. The most desirable jade came from the rivers running into the city of Khotan.

ᵟ **The Tin Road:** Early civilizations near the Mediterranean began importing tin from Central Asia around 2700 BCE. Tin was used to make bronze for weapons, tools, and household goods.

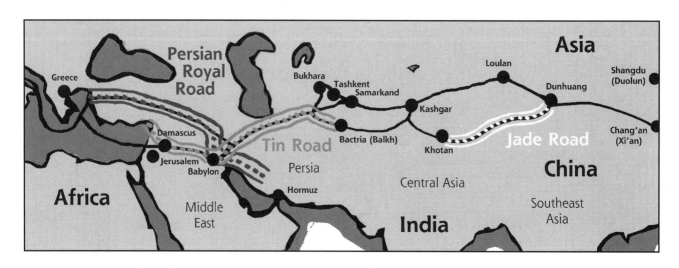

◊ **The Persian Royal Road:** From 550 BCE to 486 BCE, King Darius of Persia paved an old trading route from the Mediterranean with stone. The road was for his horse messengers. The Royal Road spanned more than 1,500 miles (2,400 kilometers). Darius's messengers could make the trip in less than 10 days.

ALEXANDER THE GREAT BRINGS GREEK CULTURE TO CENTRAL ASIA

The first major step in opening the Silk Road between the East and the West happened in 330 BCE. This was when Alexander the Great, leader of the Greek empire, conquered Persia. Alexander and his troops took control of Persian roads and pushed into Central Asia and India. This brought a long-lasting Greek influence to the region.

words to know

jade: a hard, shiny stone that is usually green. Used for jewelry and sculpture.

civilizations: communities of people that are advanced in art, science, and politics.

tin: a soft, silvery metal.

bronze: a hard, golden metal made by combining copper and tin. Used by early civilizations for tools and weapons.

MAKE YOUR OWN
Gordian Knot

One **legend** says Alexander conquered Asia by solving the puzzle of the Gordian Knot. According to a **prophecy**, whoever untied this endless knot would rule the continent. Alexander took the direct approach—he cut the knot open with his sword. Today, a "Gordian knot" means an unsolvable problem. No one knows exactly what the Gordian Knot looked like. But you can make a knot called a Turk's Head appear "endless" by joining the ends after it's tied.

supplies

ᚯ   rope, twine, or string about 3 feet (90 centimeters) long

ᚯ   scissors

ᚯ   glue and/or clear tape

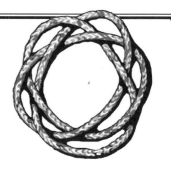

1 Start with the right end of the rope in front of you and the rest off to the left. Make a pretzel shape.

2 Bring the left end back towards the center, going over-under-over as shown.

3 Bring the left end back down, going under-over-under-over.

4 Trim the ends of the rope so they meet at the bottom of the last loop. Holding the ends together, attach with glue or wrap with tape to hold in place.

Tips for Nylon or Polyester Rope:
Pull out the inner core to make the rope more bendable. Also, you can melt the ends together and really make the knot continuous. <u>Ask an adult to help.</u> Then hold the ends about 2 inches (5 centimeters) above a candle flame.

Alexander married a princess named Roxane. She was the daughter of the chief of Bactria in Afghanistan. After making Bactria his eastern capital, Alexander built 30 new cities throughout Central Asia. The cities were filled with Greek temples and art. By the time Alexander died in 323 BCE, he had sparked a new Central Asian **culture** combining Greek, Persian, and Indian styles.

EAST MEETS WEST

The next big step in opening up the Silk Road between East and West happened around 200 years after Alexander the Great. It took place in China.

In 138 BCE, the Chinese Emperor Wudi of the Han **Dynasty** sent a **diplomat** named Zhang Qian west to make an **alliance** with the people of Central Asia. China needed help fighting the **nomads** of the **Eurasian Steppe**. But the nomads captured Zhang Qian and held him prisoner for 10 years. By the time Zhang Qian reached Central Asia, the people there had made their peace with the nomads.

words to know

legend: a story about a hero.

prophecy: telling the future.

culture: the beliefs and way of life of a group of people.

dynasty: a powerful family or group that rules for many years.

diplomat: someone who represents a country.

alliance: an agreement between two groups to help each other.

nomads: people who move their homes along regular routes according to the seasons so their animals can find grass and other plants to eat.

Eurasian Steppe: a large, flat grassland with no trees that stretches across a cool, dry region of Europe and Asia.

So instead Zhang Qian explored the wealthy and advanced civilizations left behind by Alexander the Great. When Zhang Qian returned to China, he brought the emperor wondrous tales of the cultures he had discovered to the west.

The emperor sent Zhang Qian back to learn more. He got as far as Persia. One of the things he discovered was a large, strong breed of horse in the Ferghana Valley of present-day Uzbekistan. These Celestial Horses were said to be so powerful that they sweat blood. (Scientists now believe the blood was caused by biting parasites.)

words to know

celestial: heavenly.

parasite: a small insect or other living thing that infects a larger animal and lives off it.

bamboo: a tree-like type of grass with a hollow woody stem.

tax: money charged by a government.

CELESTIAL HORSES

The Celestial Horses inspired many artists, including the eighth-century Chinese poet Tu Fu. This is one of his poems:

The Ferghana horse is famed among nomad breeds.
Lean in build, like the point of a lance;
Two ears sharp as bamboo spikes;
Four hoofs light as though born of the wind.
Heading away across the endless spaces,
Truly, you may entrust him with your life. ✛

Eventually the Chinese were able to obtain some Celestial Horses for their armies. With his new war horses, the Chinese emperor's troops drove the nomads away in 101 BCE. Meanwhile, China's new ties with Central Asia sent traders and diplomats traveling between East and West. Today Zhang Qian is called the "Father of the Silk Road."

Far to the west during this time, the Roman Empire had been busy conquering all the lands surrounding the Mediterranean Sea. Regular trade started to develop between the Roman Empire and the Chinese Empire. But the two empires didn't deal with each other directly. Instead, their goods and money were passed along by two empires that lay in between them. One was the Parthian Empire in Persia and the other was the Kushan Empire in Central Asia. Both of these empires grew rich by **taxing** traders on the Silk Road.

Fascinating Fact

The Chinese were so frightened of nomad attacks that in 221 BCE they began connecting old forts and walls along the edge of the Eurasian Steppe. This barrier grew to become the Great Wall of China.

11

Not everyone on the Silk Road was looking for riches. **Religion** sent many people out on the route as well. Missionaries traveled to distant lands to win new followers and create centers for their faith. Some believers set off on long **pilgrimages** to holy sites. And religious armies sometimes came thundering down the Silk Road to capture territory and drive out unbelievers, or to **convert** them by force. There were many different religions along the Silk Road.

Zoroastrianism: Around 650 BCE, a priest from Central Asia named Zoroaster founded a new religion. It was based on a view of life as a struggle between light and darkness. Zoroastrianism spread along the Silk Road as far as India. It became the major religion in Persia.

Judaism: Based on the worship of one God, Judaism began in the Middle East sometime before 1000 BCE. Later, many **Jews** moved into the Silk Road region from Babylon after being freed from captivity. Babylon is in modern-day Iraq. Jews helped keep trade flowing between Christians and **Muslims**.

Buddhism: Founded in northern India by a prince named Siddhartha Gautama around 500 BCE. His teachings focused on personal spiritual development. Buddhist missionaries traveled along the Silk Road to Central Asia and China. Buddhist **monks** returned to India along the Silk Road to study Buddhism at its source.

words to know

religion: a set of beliefs about reality and a god or gods.

pilgrimage: a journey to a place that is important to a religion.

convert: to convince someone to join a new religion.

Jew: a person who is Jewish, who practices Judaism.

Muslim: a person of the Islamic faith.

monk: a man who lives in a religious community and devotes himself to prayer.

Fascinating Fact

In the fifth century a **sect** of Christians in the Middle East called the Nestorians broke away from the main branches of the church. Considered **heretics**, they traveled along the Silk Road seeking **refuge**. Nestorian missionaries and settlers built communities in Central Asia and China.

Christianity: Started in the first century CE by Jews who believed Jesus Christ was the son of God. Christianity first spread through Jewish communities living near the Silk Road. Later, European missionaries used the Silk Road to spread their message.

Manichaeism: In what is now Iraq, the **prophet** Mani founded Manichaeism in the 200s CE. Manichaeism is a blend of Judaism, Christianity, Zoroastrianism, and Buddhism. Manichaen missionaries carried their religion along the Silk Road to the Kushan Empire and China.

Islam: Founded in the Middle East by the prophet Muhammad in 622 CE. Muhammad was a former trade route guide. After his death, Muslim armies moved into Central Asia. Later, during the **Crusades**, Muslims and Christians fought for control of the Middle East. But the Muslims held onto the region and its trade routes. Today most people in the Silk Road region are Muslim.

words to know

sect: a group within a religion whose beliefs are different from that of the main group.

heretic: a person who disagrees with the traditional beliefs of a religion.

refuge: a place that gives protection.

prophet: a person who claims to speak for God.

Crusades: a series of attacks by European Christians on Muslim rulers over control of the Middle East. The Crusades took place between 1095 and about 1291 CE.

13

UPS AND DOWNS ALONG THE SILK ROAD

Eventually, the Han and Roman Empires, and the empires in between, fell apart. Nomadic tribes returned to take control of western China. Trade continued, but not as freely as before.

The Tang Dynasty reunited China in 618 CE. During this dynasty, trade along the Silk Road reached new heights. A **census** in 754 CE reported 5,000 foreign merchants living in one Chinese city alone. They included Turks, Persians, Indians, Japanese, and Koreans. Trade continued to flourish throughout the dynasty, which lasted until 907 CE.

THE SILK ROAD COMES UNDER MONGOL RULE

In 1196 CE, a new force rose to power. The Mongols, like the earlier tribes of nomads, were skilled horsemen and fighters. United by the leader Genghis Khan, the Mongols conquered most of Central Asia and created the Mongol Empire.

Genghis Khan was a fierce ruler. In 1218 CE, he sent his representatives to establish trade with the Persians. But the local Persian chief had the representatives killed. Genghis Khan was so angry he set out on a path of destruction throughout Central Asia. Leading an army of 200,000, he destroyed cities and killed as many as 5 million people.

Genghis Khan also proved to be a skilled ruler. Taking the advice of local wise men, he stopped killing the people in the cities he captured. Instead, he made use of the people's skills and knowledge. He collected taxes from them to help his empire grow. His network of roads allowed Genghis to keep track of his enormous territory. It also made travel easier for merchants.

words to know

census: an official count of people living in an area.

After Genghis Khan died, his son Ogedei continued the expansion of the Mongol Empire. And so did Genghis' grandson, Kublai Khan.

GENGHIS KHAN'S EARLY LIFE

The son of a Mongol clan chief, Genghis Khan was called Temujin when he was a boy. According to legend, Temujin was only five when he was given the job of watching the tribes' herd of camels. At six he took part in wild boar hunts. When Temujin was nine, his father was murdered. Temujin, his mother, and his brothers were left to fend for themselves on the steppe.

Temujin's mother kept her family alive. But Temujin's tough spirit helped. He even killed one of his own brothers for stealing fish from the rest of the family. Temujin's reputation earned him the leadership of the Mongols, and he was given the title Genghis Khan. Even after he became emperor, his mother remained one of his most trusted advisors. ✛

Fascinating Fact

In 2003, scientists working in Central Asia found that one-eighth of all the men living in the region were probably descended from Genghis Khan.

In 1260, Kublai became the Great Khan. In 1271 he began the conquest of China and founded the Yuan Dynasty. The Mongolian Empire now spanned four regions: Mongolia and China, Persia and the Middle East, Russia, and western Asia. This was the first—and only—time the entire Silk Road was controlled by one empire. The period lasted from 1260 to 1368 CE and became known as *Pax Mongolica*, or the Mongolian Peace. Under the protection of the Mongols, trade flourished along the Silk Road. And it brought great wealth to the entire Mongol Empire.

MARCO POLO

The best-known Silk Road traveler of all time was Marco Polo. Marco was born in Venice, Italy, in 1254 CE to a family of Silk Road merchants. His father and uncle were the first Europeans to meet Kublai Khan. When he was 17, Marco set out with them for China. It took the Polos three years to reach Kublai Khan's capital. They had to cross the high Pamir Mountains and the deadly Taklamakan Desert. The emperor asked them to work for him and they stayed 17 years. Marco became one of Kublai Khan's trusted advisors.

After he returned in 1295, Marco was captured in a war with the nearby city of Genoa and thrown in prison. There he met a writer who turned Marco's stories of his travels into a book called *Description of the World*. It was one of the first eyewitness accounts ever published of China, India, and the other lands Marco visited. The book became famous throughout Europe.

Marco described the Mongol Empire as larger, richer, and more powerful than Europe. Marco talked about the great cities, the tremendous number of people, the abundance of food in the markets, the fine clothing and furniture of the people, and the magnificent homes of the wealthy. He described Kublai Khan's capital of Khanbaliq as the most magnificent city in the world. Today this city is Beijing.

DID MARCO POLO TELL THE TRUTH?

Historians still argue over Marco Polo's claims. Some point out that he never mentioned such Chinese features as tea, chopsticks, or the Great Wall. But defenders point out that Marco spent his time with the Mongol rulers, not the Chinese. And at the time of his visit the Great Wall was just mounds of earth that were falling down. Many explorers have confirmed Marco Polo's observations about the landscape and the people he met along the Silk Road. ✢

MAKE YOUR OWN
Paiza Passport

When Marco Polo traveled around the Mongol Empire, he carried a golden **paiza**, or badge. This was a passport that also entitled him to food, shelter, horses, and guides. *Paizas* were about 7 inches (18 centimeters) long, and could be round, oval, or rectangular. They had a hole or a ring at the top so they could be hung from a belt. According to the importance of the person carrying them, they were made of wood, silver, or gold. They often had the image of a lion, tiger, or dragon at the top. You can make your own model of an ancient *paiza* from gold-colored polymer clay from an art supply store. When it is baked, the clay becomes hard and metallic.

supplies

- pencil and paper
- gold or silver polymer clay
- toothpicks, plastic knives, or other shaping tools
- aluminum foil
- cookie sheet
- oven

1 Make a sketch of your *paiza*, no more than about 4 inches (10 centimeters) long. You can include pictures and writing. Don't forget to make a hole or ring at the top for hanging.

2 Soften up the clay in your hands. Then flatten it and shape it to look like the design you drew. To make raised pictures or words, make thin rolls of clay and carefully press them on to the flat shape.

3 Place your *paiza* on aluminum foil on a cookie sheet. Follow the package directions for baking the polymer clay in your oven.

Many people found Marco's fantastic stories hard to believe. His book became known as *Il Milione*, a reference to the million lies people said it contained. But Marco Polo claimed, "I have not told half of what I saw." Despite the doubts, Marco's stories sent many generations of Europeans to explore the Silk Road for themselves.

words to know

paiza: a pass for official travelers used in China under Mongol rule.

scholar: a person who is highly educated in a subject.

hajj: a religious trip to Islam's holy sites.

IBN BATTUTA

About 50 years after Marco Polo, a 20-year-old Moroccan **scholar** named Ibn Battuta also made a long journey that took him to many of the cities on the Silk Road. Starting in 1325 CE, he set out on a **hajj**, or pilgrimage, to Islam's holiest sites in the Middle East. But he didn't return home. Instead, Ibn Battuta followed the teachings of the Prophet Muhammad, who said, "Seek knowledge, even as far as China."

Over 29 years he traveled in Africa, Europe, and Asia. He covered over 75,000 miles (120,000 kilometers) throughout the Muslim world and visited Muslim communities in China. Ibn Battuta wrote about his adventures in a book titled *A Gift to Those Who Contemplate the Wonders of Cities and the Marvels of Traveling*. Today it is known as *The Rihla*, the Arab term for a travel book. ✦

MAKE YOUR OWN
Rihla Travel Journal

Traditionally, a *rihla* was about the experience of the *hajj*, or pilgrimage. Ibn Battuta's *rihla* was much more wide-ranging and interesting than the typical *rihla*. The young man hired to write down Ibn Battuta's stories even added his own poetry and bits from other people's travels. You can make your own *rihla* about a real trip or an imaginary journey you would like to take.

supplies
- δ   nice paper
- δ   your favorite pen
- δ   heavy cover paper
- δ   stapler

1 In your fanciest handwriting, write about your trip. Your *rihla* should answer these questions:

Who are you? Your name, your family, where you are from, and what you do when you're not traveling. Go ahead and brag a little. Everybody did!

Where did you go? Explain your trip's purpose, the route that you followed, and what you planned to do when you got there.

How did you get there? What types of transportation did you use? Did you hike, go by boat, take a plane? How long did the trip take? What problems did you have to overcome? What sights did you see along the way?

What did you see and do? Describe the places you stayed. Tell about the landscape, the buildings, and the weather. What were the people like? Did they have different ways of dressing or speaking? Were there any new customs you had to get used to? Did you meet anyone important or interesting? Don't forget to mention what you had to eat!

2 Illustrate your book with drawings of your adventures. You can create fancy borders, or use colored pencils.

3 When you're done, decorate a cover and staple it on. You'll have a travel journal that you can refer to and remember your special trip. Share it with others!

THE SILK ROAD FADES

By 1368 CE, the Mongol Empire had collapsed. The Chinese Ming Dynasty took over. The Mings kicked out all foreigners and closed the Silk Road. They rebuilt the Great Wall, which had become a ruin of mud and logs, making it a stronger and bigger stone barrier.

Then in 1369, a Turk called Timur the Lame tried to revive the Mongolian Empire. One of Timur's ancestors was Genghis Khan. Like his ancestor, Timur destroyed many Silk Road cities. His attacks reached India, Persia, and the Middle East. But he also built magnificent buildings in his capital city of Samarkand. Timur's empire collapsed when he died in 1405.

Fascinating Fact

Natural forces also played a part in the closing of the Silk Road. Hotter, drier weather made it impossible to grow crops in towns along the Silk Road in Central Asia. Earthquakes also damaged or destroyed many Silk Road cities.

TWO GUYS FROM QUEENS FOLLOW IN THE FOOTSTEPS OF MARCO POLO

In the early 1990s, two friends decided to retrace the route of Marco Polo. They were Denis Belliveau, a photographer, and Francis O'Donnell, a painter. Both were from Queens, New York. It took them two years to complete their journey from Venice to China and back. Like Silk Road travelers of old, they walked through the mountains and deserts of Central Asia. They were threatened by thugs and stopped at border crossings. But they met many interesting and helpful people. And they saw many of the same sights Marco Polo wrote about. In 2008, Belliveau and O'Donnell produced a TV special and a book based on their travels called *In the Footsteps of Marco Polo*. ✛

In the West, Muslim rulers in what is now Turkey started banning Christian merchants from traveling along the Silk Road. So European traders had to find other ways to reach Asia. The Italian explorer Christopher Columbus tried sailing west from Spain—but instead of Asia he found the Americas.

Portuguese explorer Vasco da Gama sailed south around Africa and reached India. Both of these explorers opened up new trade routes by sea. The days of trade and travel centering along the Silk Road were at an end.

words ^{to} know

archaeologist: a scientist who studies ancient people and their culture by digging ancient sites.

artifact: an ancient, man-made object.

scroll: a roll of paper or other material containing writing.

AFTER THE SILK ROAD

In the late 1800s, two new empires became important in the Silk Road region—Britain and Russia. Britain ruled India while Russia controlled the Eurasian Steppe. They competed for control in a rivalry known as "The Great Game."

Over the centuries, many Silk Road cities had disappeared under the desert sands. When Russia and Britain sent spies to map out the area, they began stumbling across these ancient sites. The news brought **archaeologists** from around Europe and Asia. These eager scientists brought new attention to the region. But they also disturbed important sites and took valuable **artifacts**. China put a stop to this invasion by outsiders in the early 1920s.

SIR AUREL STEIN

One of the most important modern explorers of the Silk Road was a British archaeologist named Marc Aurel Stein. In 1900, Aurel Stein gave a Chinese monk a small donation in return for thousands of Buddhist writings and paintings found in some caves outside the city of Dunhuang. Among them was a **scroll** called the Diamond Sutra, the oldest printed book ever found. Aurel Stein's discoveries are now in museums and libraries in England and India. ✦

COUNTRIES OF THE SILK ROAD REGION TODAY

Today the Silk Road region is made up of many independent countries, as well as areas controlled by larger nations.

ᕛ Turkey, Syria, Iran, Iraq, and Afghanistan became independent countries around the start of the 1900s.

ᕛ Turkmenistan, Uzbekistan, Tajikistan, Kyrgyzstan, and Kazakhstan gained independence from Russian control when the Soviet Union broke apart in 1991.

ᕛ China now includes the **autonomous** regions of Xinjiang Uighur, Tibet, and Inner Mongolia.

Other countries connected to the Silk Road by trade routes include Italy, Egypt, India, Pakistan, Sri Lanka, Russia, and Japan.

words to know

autonomous: self-governing.

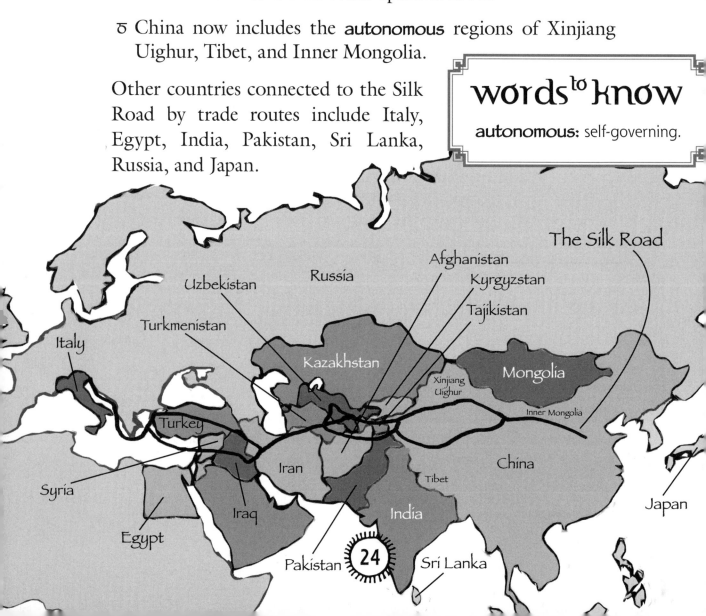

chapter 2

Wonders from Afar:
Trade Goods

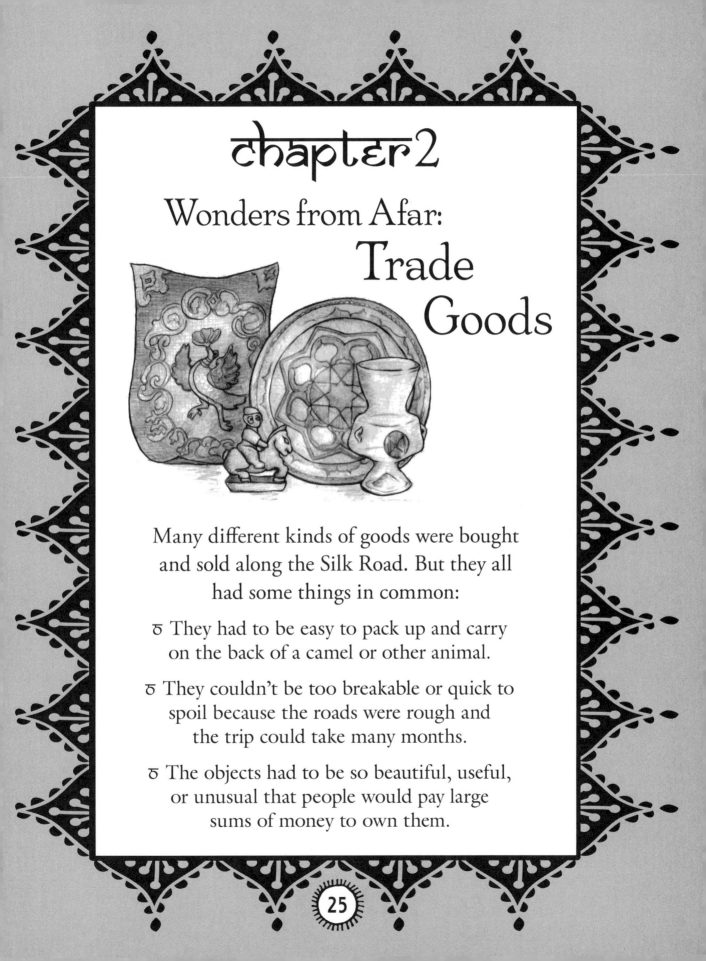

Many different kinds of goods were bought and sold along the Silk Road. But they all had some things in common:

ᚦ They had to be easy to pack up and carry on the back of a camel or other animal.

ᚦ They couldn't be too breakable or quick to spoil because the roads were rough and the trip could take many months.

ᚦ The objects had to be so beautiful, useful, or unusual that people would pay large sums of money to own them.

This wasn't because the merchants were greedy. Traders took big risks and spent a lot of time, money, and effort bringing goods from one end of the Silk Road to the other. They had to feed themselves and their animals. They had to hire guides to lead them through the most difficult stretches. Often there were taxes, tolls, fees, and bribes.

Most Silk Road goods passed from one trader to another several times before they reached their final destination. Every time one merchant sold his goods to another, the price went up. As a result, only the most expensive items were traded along the Silk Road.

These expensive items fell into a few categories. There were fine decorative handicrafts like silk, which took skill, training, and special materials to produce. There were precious stones and metals. And there were plants, animals, foods, and medicines only found in certain parts of the world. These were the types of things merchants hoped would make them a nice **profit** at the end of their journey.

Fascinating Fact

In 1340 CE, the Italian merchant Francesco Pegolotti wrote a guidebook for traders headed to China. His tips included how to lower taxes on the road by offering custom-house officials "something of a present in goods or money"—in other words, a bribe.

words to know

profit: the extra money or goods kept after paying costs of doing business.

commodity: a product made, grown, or gathered for sale.

sericulture: the process of making silk.

filament: a single thin thread.

bolt: a roll of fabric.

SILK

Silk was hard to make, easy to carry, and beautiful. It was one of the most profitable **commodities** traded between East and West. Part of its value was its rarity. For centuries, only the Chinese knew the secret of **sericulture**, or silkmaking.

Silkmaking began in China around 2600 BCE. According to legend, it was invented by Lei-zu, the wife of the emperor. One day Lei-zu was enjoying a cup of tea and playing with a silkworm cocoon. Suddenly her hand slipped and the cocoon fell into the hot tea. As she tried to scoop it out, the silk **filament** that made up the cocoon began to unwind in the boiling water. Lei-zu realized this delicate filament could be spun into thread and woven into a beautiful cloth. This story may or may not be true. But according to Chinese tradition silkmaking was done by women in every Chinese household, even the richest.

Fascinating Fact

Silk was so valuable in China that taxes could be paid in **bolts** of silk cloth.

Regular silk trade with the West began during the Han Dynasty in the second century BCE. At first in ancient Rome, silk was so expensive that even wealthy people wore only a tiny piece sewn to their clothing.

27

But by 380 CE one Roman wrote, "The use of silk which was once confined to the nobility has now spread to all classes without distinction, even to the lowest." Romans spent so much money on silk that it threatened the entire economy. Years earlier, in 14 CE, the Roman Senate had tried to pass a law banning men from wearing silk. No one followed it.

HOW SILK IS MADE

The silkworm is the **larva**, or caterpillar stage, of the silkworm moth. Silkworms are raised in baskets. They begin as tiny eggs no bigger than poppy seeds. After they hatch, the tiny worms are fed mulberry leaves, which is the only food they will eat. They spend all their time eating until they are big enough to spin **cocoons**.

To make their cocoons, silkworms produce a sticky substance from their mouths. This substance becomes a very long, strong filament. The filament from one cocoon can be as much as half a mile long!

Silkmakers first drop the cocoons into vats of boiling water. This kills the silkworms inside before they turn into moths and break the valuable filament. While the cocoons are floating in the vat, a silkmaker carefully gathers the ends of several filaments as they begin to unwind. The silkmaker pulls and gently winds them onto a large wheel. The separate filaments are then twisted together to make a thicker strand of thread. Finally, the thread is woven into cloth. ✛

The silk trade was so profitable for China that smuggling silkworm eggs out of the country was punished by death. But stories say that in 440 CE the ruler of Khotan in Central Asia convinced his bride coming from China to hide silkworm eggs in her headdress. Later, in 552 CE, other people from Khotan smuggled silkworms out of China by stashing them in hollow bamboo walking sticks. But even after silkmaking spread to other countries, Chinese silk was always considered the best.

words to know

larva: the worm form of an insect.

cocoon: protective covering made by an insect larva.

domesticated: bred to be easier for humans to take care of.

Fascinating Fact

Originally wild silkworms lived in mulberry trees. But over time the Chinese bred silkworms that could not fly. These **domesticated** silkworms were easier to raise indoors. But the worms are very sensitive. They have to be protected from loud noises and cold breezes. Even strong smells like fish, meat, or sweat must be avoided. Within a month, they weigh 10,000 times as much as when they hatched.

MAKE YOUR OWN
Embroidered Butterfly

You can use a simple satin stitch to embroider a tiny butterfly. Find an old silk blouse or handkerchief at a used clothing store. If you know how to sew, you can also recycle an old piece of silk into an embroidered good luck drawstring purse.

supplies

ᛜ silk or other soft fabric to embroider

ᛜ scissors

ᛜ 2 or more colors of embroidery floss

ᛜ tapestry needle or other large, easy-to-handle needle

1 Cut a piece of floss about 2 feet (60 centimeters) long. Put one end through the eye of the needle (the hole). Pull it through. Knot the two ends of the floss together.

2 To make the first stitch, push the point of the needle up through the fabric from underneath. Pull until the knot is gently resting against the fabric. Push the point back down into the fabric about a half inch (1 centimeter) away. This is your first stitch.

3 Make a second stitch alongside the first, but shorter. Then make a third and fourth stitch right next to those, getting smaller each time. Your stitches will form a small pyramid. This is one wing of the butterfly.

4 Leave a space one stitch wide for the body, and start the other wing. Make a small stitch, then three larger stitches, mirroring the first wing. Turn the fabric over to the side with the knot. Make a knot in the floss next to the fabric. Trim off the excess.

5 Thread the needle with a different color floss. Make one stitch between the two wings for the body. Make two more stitches in the shape of a "V" for the butterfly's antennae. When finished, knot and trim off the excess.

Fascinating Fact

In China, silkworm larvae are sometimes eaten boiled or barbecued.

SILK EMBROIDERY

Silk thread was used in **embroidery** as well. Girls in China traditionally made embroidered silk pouches to give as gifts. Sometimes they filled the pouches with herbs for protection or good luck. Silk embroidery was also used to create full-sized portraits or landscapes. Embroidered "paintings" of Buddha, a thousand years old, have been found in ancient cave temples.

words to know

embroidery: the art of making pictures or designs using threads sewn onto fabric.

CARPETS

Next to silk, elaborate carpets from Central Asia may have been the most highly prized goods traded on the Silk Road. Carpets were important to the Central Asian way of life. It was said that: "Water is a man's life, a horse is his wings, and a carpet is his soul."

According to Marco Polo "the best and handsomest carpets in the world" were made in the Anatolia region of present-day Turkey. Anatolian carpets became famous throughout the Middle East, Persia, and India. They even set off a carpet craze in Europe.

Persia, Turkey, Turkmenistan, India, Mongolia, Tibet, and China also had their own carpet-making traditions. Each region had its own symbols and designs. For example, designs featuring ram's horns and water symbolized life and good fortune. Flowers meant fertility and plenty. And spiders, symbolizing evil spirits, were put in the borders of carpets to guard against the real thing.

GLASSWARE

Surprisingly, one of the most popular Silk Road trade goods was not very easy to transport. European glass was almost as popular in China as Chinese silk was in Europe. So traders packed up fragile bowls, bottles, and jars and hoped for the best. If they were lucky, enough glass made it to the other end of the route in one piece for merchants to turn a profit.

The process of making glass from **molten** sand and other ingredients was discovered around 3500 BCE. According to one ancient story, traders from North Africa were cooking over a fire on a sandy beach.

> ### Fascinating Fact
>
> In 2001, the world's largest handmade carpet was created in honor of Turkmenistan's 10th anniversary of independence. It measured nearly 1,000 square feet (300 square meters) and weighed more than a ton. Forty weavers— all women—worked for eight months to produce it.

When they rested their hot pots on blocks of salt, the salt melted. It mixed with the sand below and formed chunks of glass.

At first the technique was used to make glass beads, which were considered the equal of gemstones. The oldest glass objects ever found in China were "evil eye" beads from the Mediterranean. These date back to 550–380 BCE.

words to know

molten: made liquid by heat.

glassblowing: making glass bowls or bottles by blowing into a lump of hot, soft glass through a long metal tube.

mosque: a Muslim house of worship.

The Egyptians learned to make glass pots using molds around 1500 BCE. **Glassblowing** was invented in Syria around the first century BCE. New and different shapes could be made more quickly than ever before. Soon the Romans were shipping glass bottles, cups, and bowls to the far reaches of their empire and beyond.

Venice became the center of European glassmaking. In 1291 CE, the city moved its glassmaking furnaces to the nearby island of Murano. This helped prevent the spread of fires—and the spread of the city's glassmaking secrets. Murano's famous glass workshops were soon making lamps for **mosques** throughout the Muslim world.

MAKE YOUR OWN
Felt Rug

The people of Kyrgyzstan in Central Asia are famous for their felt rugs, known as *shyrdak* rugs. These rugs are made by placing clumps of wool together, and then wetting, pressing, and rolling up the clumps until they form a thick mat. *Shyrdaks* are brightly colored and have many designs. Some of the designs have specific meanings. For instance, birds in flight symbolize a wish for dreams to come true, while a ram's horn represents wealth. You can make a replica of a Central Asian felt rug using pre-made felt pieces.

Supplies

ᴆ   3 or more felt pieces in at least two colors

ᴆ   paper and pencil

ᴆ   scissors

ᴆ   glue

1 Using the paper and pencil, sketch out the design you'd like to make on your carpet. Cut out the shapes to make pattern pieces.

2 Use the paper pattern pieces to cut out pieces of felt.

3 Take a rectangular piece of felt and lay it out for the background. Glue the felt shapes onto the background. Put a thin line of glue around the edges of each piece, but don't soak through the felt.

Fascinating Fact

The oldest known woven rug, the Pazyryk Carpet, was discovered in a frozen burial mound on the Eurasian Steppe. It dates from the 400s BCE. But the skill used in making it is the same as in modern carpets.

4 Your felt carpet can be hung up as a wall decoration, just as the nomads do in their tents.

Evil Eye Glass Marble

supplies

- clear flat glass marbles
- white paper
- permanent markers
- scissors
- clear-drying glue
- round ceramic magnet

Flat "evil eye" glass beads called *nazar boncugu* are a favorite good luck charm in Turkey. *Nazar boncugu* are supposed to reflect back the evil wishes of people who are jealous of someone's good fortune. Today they are made in any color. But the classic *nazar boncugu* has a black dot in the middle, a yellow "iris" for the colored part of the eye, and a "white of the eye" area surrounded by a ring of dark blue.

Nazar boncugu are hung over doorways and from rear-view mirrors in cars. They are pinned to babies' clothing and stuck on refrigerators as magnets. You can make your own *nazar boncugu* from flat glass marbles sold for flower arranging.

1 Put the marble flat on the paper and trace around it to make a guide. Draw the evil eye design within the circle on the paper. Use the markers to color in the evil eye design. Cover your work area, because the ink may bleed through the paper. Cut around the outside of the circle.

2 Turn the marble round side down. Spread the glue on the flat side of the marble. Then place the drawing—colored side facing the glass—to the marble. Let sit until completely dry. Glue the round ceramic magnet to the back if you want to display it on your refrigerator.

PORCELAIN

Another popular trade good was the beautiful but delicate dishware known as **porcelain**. The Persians called it "china," their name for the country it came from. Although breakable like glass, it was so highly prized in the West that traders took the risk. The Chinese invented porcelain around the seventh or eighth century CE using a special kind of clay found only in China. Porcelain plates, bowls, and teapots were so thin that light could shine through them. In the 1400s CE in Italy, people believed that the **glaze** on a porcelain bowl or cup would crack if poison was poured into it, warning of danger. ✛

words to know

porcelain: a type of white pottery that is thin, smooth, and shiny.

glaze: a glassy coating that waterproofs and decorates pottery.

preserve: make food last longer.

sacred: a place or object that is worshipped.

incense: a material that is burned to produce a pleasant smell.

SPICES

Up until modern times, spices were more than just a way to liven up bland meals. They were used for medicines, perfumes, and to **preserve** food. Some spices were considered **sacred** and burned as **incense** during religious ceremonies. And like some other Silk Road trade goods, spices were sometimes used in place of money. Spices traveled both east and west on the Silk Road. China and Rome both exported salt, while India exported pepper in both directions.

SPICES TRADED ON THE SILK ROAD AND ITS CONNECTING ROUTES

SPICE:	COMES FROM:	SOURCE PLANT:	USED FOR:
sesame	Europe, Middle East	seed of an herb plant	bread, candy, oil, medicine
coriander	Europe, Middle East	seed of the cilantro plant	preserving sausages
saffron	Bukhara in Central Asia	part of the crocus flower	orange coloring, perfume
cinnamon	China	bark of the cassia tree	incense, sweets
ginger	China, India	root of reed plant	tea, stomach medicine
cumin	China	seed of parsley-type herb	preserving meats
nutmeg	Southeast Asia	seed of an evergreen tree	love potions, headache medicine
cloves	Southeast Asia	unopened flower buds from evergreen tree	breath sweetener

Fascinating Fact

When a tribe called the Goths captured Rome in 410 CE, they demanded a payment of 3,000 pounds of black pepper.

Fascinating Fact

The unofficial slogan of the U.S. Postal Service—"Neither snow, nor rain, nor heat, nor darkness of night prevents these couriers from completing their designated stages with utmost speed"—was first said about King Darius' horse messengers by the Greek historian Herodotus.

The overland spice trade began in the Middle East around 3000 BCE. By 300 CE, Arab spice merchants were trading with China and Europe. But they kept the source of their spices a secret. They even made up stories of dangerous monsters and other perils faced by spice gatherers.

Eventually the Greeks and Romans began importing spices on their own, rather than buying them from Arab traders. But they too kept their true sources a secret—until Marco Polo sailed home from China to Venice by way of the **Spice Route**. He revealed that many spices actually came from India and the Spice Islands of Southeast Asia, not Africa or the Middle East. By the late 1400s, Vasco da Gama and other explorers were sailing directly to the trading ports of Asia, avoiding the land route and its costly middlemen.

words to know

Spice Route: a route by sea from the Spice Islands of Southeast Asia to India, Africa, and Europe.

Healthy Spiced Tea

supplies

- 1 mug or cup
- 1 teabag black tea (can use decaffeinated)
- finely-ground black pepper
- boiling water
- 1 teaspoon honey

One of the most common spices in the kitchen today, black pepper has also been used as medicine. Its germ-killing properties have made it useful for making familiar sandwich meats like salami, which keep a long time without spoiling. And some people brew pepper into a tea for colds, congestion, sore throats, and fatigue. Here's an easy recipe for Black Pepper Tea.

1 Put the teabag in your mug or cup. Add a pinch of pepper. Pour in boiling water. Let sit for 3–5 minutes.

2 Remove the teabag. Stir in honey. Enjoy!

Fascinating Fact

The Greek writer Herodotus believed that cinnamon came from the nests of giant birds, who were lured down with pieces of cut-up oxen.

chapter 3

Over Mountains, Deserts, and Seas

Before heading out onto the interconnecting byways of the Silk Road, travelers had to decide which route to take. They could go partly by sea or stay strictly on land.

They could make the difficult crossing through the mountains and the deserts. Or they could go around them and risk attack by hostile tribes on the grassy plains. They could head for a rest stop offering food and shelter, or avoid the towns and save money. Sometimes they had to detour around war zones, closed borders, or natural disasters. But no matter what route they chose, Silk Road travelers had a long, challenging, often dangerous journey ahead of them. But there were many wonders to be seen, as well.

CARAVANS

Silk Road travelers had to be prepared. Even though there were **oasis** towns all along the route, travelers might spend days between towns without water or shelter.

words to know

oasis: a green area with water in a dry region or desert. The plural of oasis is oases.

caravan: a group of travelers and pack animals on a journey.

Silk Road merchants traveled in groups, called **caravans**. These were long lines of pack animals—usually camels—that carried equipment and trade goods. A typical caravan might consist of dozens or even thousands of animals. The animals carried packs slung on either side of their bodies. These packs contained tents and personal belongings, and enough food and water to last the travelers from one oasis to another.

Fascinating Fact

Some caravans brought along dogs for protection against thieves and wild animals like wolves, leopards, and cheetahs.

It was very important to have experienced caravan leaders. These were local people who served as guides and translators. Guides knew the best places to camp and they could deal with the local people. And they wouldn't lose the trail in a storm.

Depending on the terrain, a caravan could cover about 20 miles (32 kilometers) in a day. Each day when the caravan stopped, the camels were unloaded. All the cargo was piled up in a circle around the tents for protection. Guards kept watch at night to protect the valuable merchandise.

On some desert routes in the Middle East, caravans hired a local tribesman to come along. This person served as a *rafiq*, or "human passport." In exchange for goods or money, the *rafiq* guaranteed that the caravan would be allowed to pass through his territory safely.

words to know

dromedary camel: a one-humped camel native to North Africa and Southern Asia.

Bactrian camel: a two-humped camel native to the Gobi Desert of China.

yak: a large, longhaired ox with curved horns that is native to Tibet.

mule: an animal that is a cross between a horse and a donkey.

THE CAMEL AND OTHER PACK ANIMALS

Some historians say it was the camel that made the Silk Road possible. A camel can travel more than 2 miles (4 kilometers) an hour. That's as fast as a horse or an ox pulling a wagon. But a camel doesn't need a wagon. It can carry 300–500 pounds on its back.

Unlike the horse or ox, the camel can live on the sparse desert vegetation. And it can travel for up to two weeks without water, living off the fat stored in its humps. The camel is also resistant to heat. Its body temperature can rise 10 degrees Fahrenheit (12 degrees Celsius) without breaking a sweat.

Camels were first used as pack animals in Syria around the seventh century BCE. In the western part of the Silk Road region, **dromedary camels** were best suited for crossing the hot deserts. In the east, where cold, rough weather was common, long-haired **Bactrian camels** were used. Dromedaries can be identified by their one hump, while Bactrian camels have two.

Caravans sometimes used other animals as well. Horses were preferred on the Eurasian Steppe, where water and grassland were available. In mountainous regions like Tibet, **yaks** carried salt over the cold, high mountain passes. And on narrow mountain trails, donkeys and **mules** often carried smaller loads. ✛

THE MAIN SILK ROAD ROUTES

As it passed from Europe to Persia to Central Asia to China, the Silk Road frequently split off into different paths. These paths joined up again farther along the way. A traveler heading east from Europe had a choice of two routes to Persia. One crossed the deserts of the Middle East. The other passed through what is now Turkey. But in the mountains of Persia, there was only one road travelers could take. This gave Persia complete control over who could pass along the Silk Road.

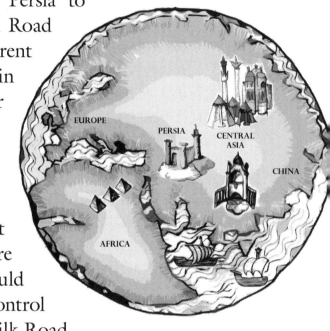

In Central Asia, travelers could pass south through Bactria or north through Bukhara before reaching the Pamir Mountains. The Persians called the Pamirs "The Roof of the World" because they were so high. Over the Pamirs was the Tarim **Basin**. Here the route split. The northern Silk Road followed the Tien Shan Mountains. The southern Silk Road stayed close to the Kunlun Mountains (part of the Tibetan **Plateau**).

words to know

basin: a bowl-shaped area of rocky ground.

plateau: a large, raised area of the earth.

corridor: a narrow pathway through land that is hard to cross.

canyon: a deep, narrow valley with steep sides.

44

THE EURASIAN STEPPE ROUTE

The shortest and easiest Silk Road route of them all was also the least used. The Eurasian Steppe Route ran through what is now Mongolia and Russia. It avoided the toughest mountains and deserts of the other routes. About 5,000 miles (8,000 kilometers) long, it steered north through mostly flat and level grassland. In fact, it was the only route that could be crossed by cart. But the steppe was also home to many warlike tribes. During the *Pax Mongolia*, when Mongols kept the peace, travelers on the Eurasian Steppe Route were given protection from attack. But at other times in history the route was too dangerous for most traders to cross. ✛

Either way, travelers had to make their way around the lifeless Taklamakan Desert at the center of the Tarim Basin. The northern route offered more cities where traders could rest and stock up on supplies. And the southern route avoided a particularly harsh stretch where the Taklamakan and the Gobi Deserts meet. The two routes joined up again at the Hexi (or Gansu) Corridor, a narrow strip of fertile land between the Gobi and the high Tibetan Plateau. It led to the heart of China. The Silk Road crossed many different kinds of terrain. From frozen mountain ranges to barren deserts, each presented its own challenge.

Fascinating Fact

In Persia, the Silk Road passed through the Buzgala Defile, a canyon so narrow that it was sometimes blocked off with a set of iron gates.

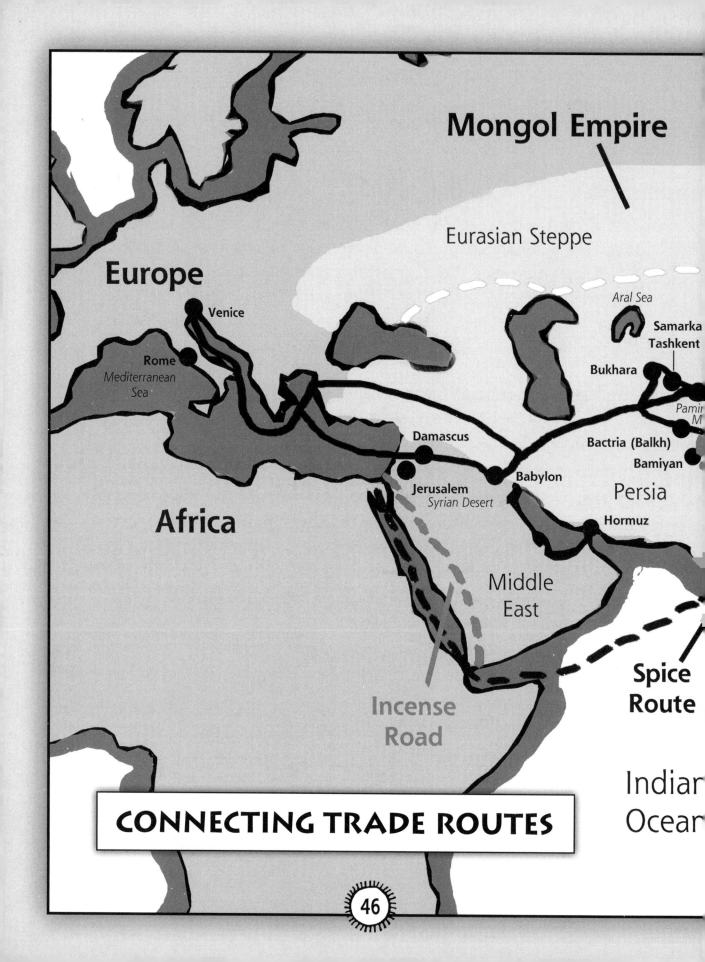

Mongol Empire

Eurasian Steppe

Europe

Venice

Aral Sea

Samarka
Tashkent

Rome
Mediterranean
Sea

Bukhara

Pamir
M

Damascus

Bactria (Balkh)

Jerusalem
Syrian Desert

Babylon

Bamiyan

Africa

Persia

Hormuz

Middle
East

Spice
Route

Incense
Road

Indiar
Ocear

CONNECTING TRADE ROUTES

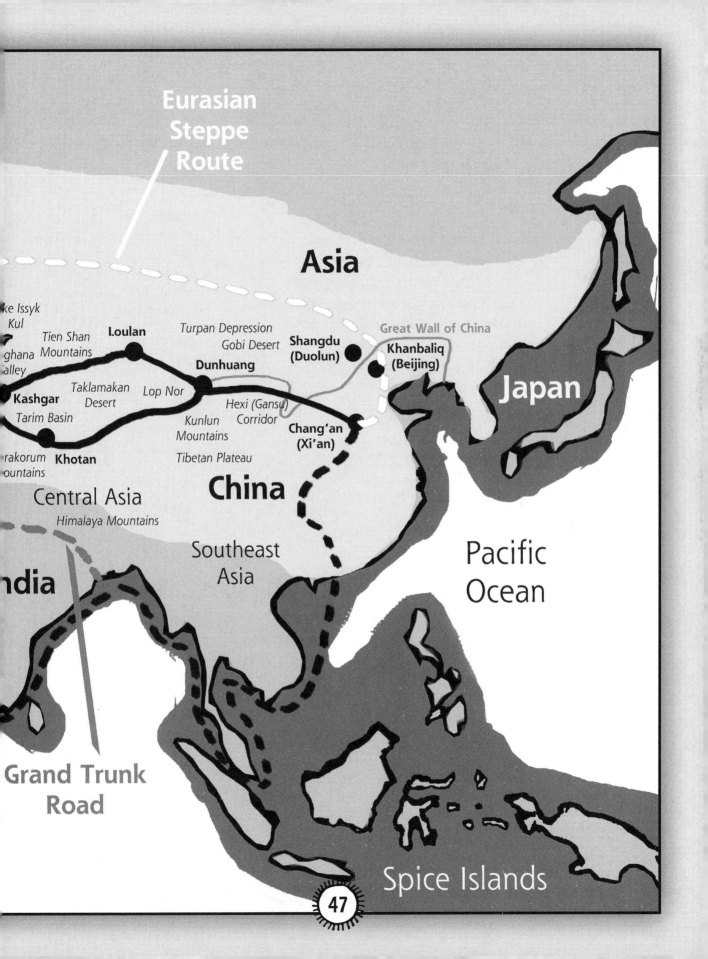

MAKE YOUR OWN
"Ancient" Silk Road Map

Maps from the time of the Silk Road were hand drawn and elaborately illustrated. You can make your own version of a Silk Road map on regular paper, and then make it look ancient. When it's finished, you can roll up your map and tie it with a ribbon, or display it in a frame.

supplies

- white paper
- pencil
- permanent markers
- baking pan or cookie sheet big enough to hold the paper
- cup of coffee (or very strong tea)
- sponge or paintbrush
- oven

1 Decide what you would like to include on your map, such as the Silk Road, other trade routes, or Marco Polo's path. Look at the maps in this book or find ancient maps to copy.

2 Using the pencil, sketch your map on the paper. Then go over your lines with the permanent marker.

3 To get a rough, aged effect, tear the edges off the paper, being careful not to remove any important parts of the map. You can also tear small holes in it.

4 Crumple up the piece of paper as tightly as you can. Then flatten it out again.

5 Lay the paper in the baking pan. Brush on coffee, making the edges and holes extra dark. Sprinkle wet coffee grounds to make dark spots.

6 Turn the oven to 200 degrees Fahrenheit (95 degrees Celsius). Put the pan in the oven until the paper is dry, about 5–10 minutes. Watch that it doesn't burn.

SILK ROAD CONNECTIONS

The Silk Road was part of a larger web of trade routes, including:

ᚣ **The Spice Route:** Linking China, Southeast Asia, and India by sea, the Spice Route met up with the Silk Road in the Middle East.

ᚣ **The Incense Road:** Running from the tip of the Arabian Peninsula to the Mediterranean, the Incense Road connected to the Spice Route in several places.

ᚣ **The Grand Trunk Road:** Joining the Silk Road in the Himalaya Mountains, (the highest in the world), the Grand Trunk Road crossed India to reach the Indian Ocean. ✛

FLATLANDS ALONG THE SILK ROAD

Where low-lying sections of the Silk Road had plenty of oasis towns, traveling was relatively easy. Caravans didn't have to worry about having enough water to drink or grass for their animals to eat. But drier sections were still hazardous.

ᚣ **The Tarim Basin** to the west is an oval-shaped lowland surrounded by some of the highest mountains in the world. About 800 miles (1,300 kilometers) long and 400 miles (650 kilometers) wide, only its rim can support people and towns. In the center are the Taklamakan Desert and the Lop Nor, a salty marsh.

THE TURPAN DEPRESSION

At the edge of the Tarim Basin is the Turpan Depression, the second lowest place on Earth. It sits at 505 feet (154 meters) below sea level. No rivers reach it. But an ancient system of underground wells and canals called a *karez* collects water seeping down from the nearby Tien Shan Mountains. This watering system has turned the Turpan Depression into a center for grape growing. ✛

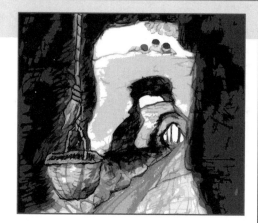

ᴆ **The Hexi Corridor** is part of the old Jade Road in western China. This narrow strip of land 600 miles (1,000 kilometers) long is bordered by the Gobi Desert to the north and the Tibetan Plateau to the south. Thanks to rain and melted snow running off the Qilian Mountains, it is dotted with many green and fertile oases. It is still famous for its melons.

DESERTS ALONG THE SILK ROAD

Most of the Silk Road was **arid**. Wherever there was enough water to survive, an oasis town would be built, but in between were the forbidding deserts.

ᴆ **The Syrian Desert** in the Middle East was not as harsh as other Silk Road deserts. There was enough water available for people and animals, so several routes passed through here.

ᚭ **The Taklamakan Desert**, unlike the nearby Gobi, is very sandy and almost totally lifeless. Some say that its name means "You go in but you don't come out." According to Marco Polo, it took several days to get from one oasis to the next in this desert.

ᚭ **The Gobi Desert** is large and rocky, about 1,000 miles (1,600 kilometers) long and 500 miles (800 kilometers) wide. It lies 5,000 feet (1,520 meters) above sea level, so it also gets very cold. Still, it contains enough water in wells and small lakes for people and animals to live there.

MOUNTAIN RANGES ALONG THE SILK ROAD

Mountain paths on the Silk Road were often so steep and narrow that people and animals were in danger of falling. And **mountain passes** were so high that the air was extremely thin. Bad weather and sudden storms meant travelers often didn't make it across.

ᚭ **The Tien Shan** mountain range rises 24,406 feet (7,439 meters) into the air. The Chinese call them the Celestial Mountains. The Tien Shan run along the northern edge of the Tarim Basin for 1,500 miles (2,400 kilometers). For centuries, their melting **glaciers** have provided water to the towns below.

words to know

arid: dry.

mountain pass: a lower place between two mountains where it is easier to cross.

glacier: a large river of ice that moves down a mountain slope.

The **Pamir Mountains** at the western end of the Tarim Basin are where some of the world's highest mountain ranges meet. These are the Tien Shan, Karakoram, Kunlun, Hindu Kush, and Himalayas. China, Tajikistan, Afghanistan, and Pakistan meet here.

Marco Polo crossed the Pamirs over a pass roughly 18,000 feet (5,500 meters) high. He wrote: "for the whole twelve days you see no houses, neither vegetation; food should be brought by yourself. There are no birds here because it is high and cold. Because of terrible cold, fire is not as bright and not of the color like in other places."

However, it wasn't the cold that made the fire look different. It was the thinner air. At that **altitude**, there is less **oxygen** in the air for people and animals to breathe and for the fire to burn.

words to know

altitude: the height of land above the level of the sea.

oxygen: a gas in the air that animals need to breathe to stay alive.

altitude sickness: a condition that occurs in very high mountains where the air is thin. Too little oxygen in the blood makes a person feel light-headed and nauseous.

Fascinating Fact

The Karakoram Highway is the highest paved road in the world. The highway follows a branch of the old Silk Road between China and Pakistan. Completed in 1986, it took 20 years to build and climbs to a height of over 15,000 feet (4,700 meters).

supplies

- ☼ small tea candle or votive candle
- ☼ fireproof plate to hold the candle
- ☼ matches
- ☼ 3 clear glass jars, small, medium, and large
- ☼ clock with second hand
- ☼ paper and pencil

The reason Marco Polo thought his campfire looked different in the thin air of the Pamir Mountains is that fire needs oxygen to burn. When a material like wood or candle wax becomes hot enough, it begins to smoke. If the chemicals in the smoke combine with oxygen in the air, new chemicals are formed. This process also gives off heat and light, which we see as fire. Lots of oxygen, big flames. Less oxygen, smaller flames. You can test this process with a simple experiment. For safety, you'll need an adult helper.

Fascinating Fact

The Chinese called the Pamirs the "Onion Mountains." They thought the onions that grew there caused them to feel light-headed and nauseous. But the real reason was probably the lower amounts of oxygen in the air at that height, which can cause **altitude sickness.**

1 Set the candle on the plate. Have your adult helper light the candle. Notice the height and color of the flame.

2 Turn the largest jar upside down and lower it over the candle until it is resting on the plate.

3 Note the time. Write down how long it takes for the flame to go out.

4 Repeat with the medium and small jars. Which flame goes out the quickest? Why do you think this happens?

RIVERS, LAKES, AND SEAS ALONG THE SILK ROAD

> ### Fascinating Fact
>
> Since the hulls of the stitched ships were not rigid, they did not crack open when they hit a rock.

Marco Polo and his family began their journey from Europe to China by sea. Leaving Venice, they sailed across the Mediterranean to the Middle East, near Jerusalem. From there they went by land to the city of Hormuz on the Persian Gulf. In Hormuz they looked for a ship to take them the rest of the way to China.

After seeing what the port had to offer, they changed their minds. "Their ships are wretched affairs," Marco wrote, "and many of them get lost; for they have no iron fastenings, and are only stitched together with twine made from the husk of the Indian nut." So the Polos made the rest of the trip by land. Years later, Kublai Khan gave them ships for the return voyage. The trip by sea took them through the Spice Islands of the Pacific Ocean, around the coast of India and back to Hormuz.

Most Silk Road travelers stuck to land routes. But rivers, lakes, and seas were important to the people of the Silk Road region for other reasons as well.

ᛏ **The Aral Sea** was the world's fourth largest lake when Marco Polo passed by on his way from Persia to the Pamirs. It was a major oasis on the Silk Road, with fishing towns and markets lining its shores. In modern times the water flowing into the Aral Sea has been cut off, and today the lake is in danger of disappearing altogether.

ᛏ **Lake Issyk Kul** was another major stop for traders. Nestorian Christians who came along the Silk Road from the Middle East founded a large community here. The name Issyk Kul means "warm lake." This lake never freezes over, even though it is high in the Tien Shan Mountains. Fed by hot springs, Issyk Kul is also very large—2,407 square miles (6,236 square kilometers)—and very deep—2,192 feet (668 meters), almost half a mile. But it's probably the salty water that keeps it ice free.

RISING WATERS OF ISSYK KUL

Many springs and streams flow into Issyk Kul, but there are no outlets to drain the water. Over time the waters have risen. Archaeologists recently discovered the remains of cities under the lake's surface. They found coins, gold bars, and bronze cauldrons as old as 2,500 years. ✢

ᛏ **The White Jade and Black Jade Rivers** were the sources of the jade that made the city of Khotan a busy destination for traders from China. The stones are really white and green. Carried down by the rushing water from the nearby mountains, they ranged in size from pebbles to boulders.

USE TABLE SALT TO
Keep Water From Freezing

One of the reasons Lake Issyk Kul doesn't freeze is because of its salty water. When water freezes, it changes from a liquid to a solid. We call the solid form of water "ice." Normally, this happens at a freezing point of 32 degrees Fahrenheit (0 degrees Celsius). But if you dissolve another substance, such as salt, into water, it makes it harder for the water to change into a solid shape. You can test this by seeing how quickly fresh water freezes compared to salt water.

supplies

- ♁ 2 identical cups (more if you want to try different amounts of salt)
- ♁ paper and pencil
- ♁ water
- ♁ salt
- ♁ spoon
- ♁ freezer
- ♁ clock
- ♁ small outdoor thermometer (optional)

1 Mark one of the cups "F" for fresh and the other "S" for salt.

2 Fill both cups partway with water. Make sure they each contain the same amount of water.

3 Add 3–6 spoonfuls of salt to the cup marked "S." Stir until the salt is completely dissolved.

4 Place both cups in the same part of the freezer. Make a note of the time.

5 Check the cups every hour or so to see if there has been any change. Write down the time and what you see.

6 Keep checking after the fresh water freezes. If you have a thermometer, stick it in the salt water for a minute to see how cold it is. Does it go below the freezing point of water? Does the salt water ever freeze?

ANIMAL LIFE ON THE SILK ROAD

Domesticated animals like camels, horses, sheep, and silkworms were an important part of life on the Silk Road. But so were wild animals. Some, such as ostriches from Africa, were even sold by merchants. The Chinese called ostriches "camel birds" because of their long, knobby camel-like legs! Other animals from the Silk Road region include:

σ **Dinosaurs:** Dinosaur fossils are constantly being found in the Gobi Desert and elsewhere on the Silk Road. The Chinese thought dinosaur bones came from dragons. They ground them up and used them as medicine for dizziness and leg cramps.

σ **Marco Polo Sheep:** Marco Polo was the first European to describe these sheep. They live in the Pamir Mountains and can weigh more than 300 pounds (135 kilograms). Their curly horns are the longest of any animal—over 6 feet (2 meters).

σ **Musk Deer:** Musk deer live in the mountains of China, Central Asia, and Mongolia. They are only about the size of small dogs. But they are valuable to local hunters. Their strong scent is a traditional ingredient in perfumes and medicines.

σ **Tigers:** Siberian Tigers in Russia and Caspian Tigers in Central Asia were recently found to be nearly identical. Scientists now believe that long ago the tigers migrated through China on the path that became the Silk Road. ✜

PLANT LIFE ON THE SILK ROAD

Fruits and vegetables are plentiful around oases on the Silk Road, but plants are scarce in the drier regions in between. On the steppe and in the desert, there are so few trees that the only part of a house that is made of wood is the door.

Of course, trees like the mulberry, which supply food for silkworms, have played a very important role in Silk Road history. Some other noteworthy trees include:

ᕭ **Willows:** The thin flexible branches of red willow trees were used to make the framework for mud buildings in Silk Road cities like Loulan. Willow branches were also used for the first version of the Great Wall.

ᕭ **Lacquer Trees:** The lacquer tree from China is related to poison ivy. You can get a severe skin rash by touching its thick, milky sap. But the sap is highly valued because it can be used as a hard, shiny coating on wood furniture. Red and black lacquerware products were very popular on the Silk Road. The seeds and leaves of lacquer trees were also used in Chinese medicine.

chapter 4

Peoples of the Silk Road

Over thousands of years, the Silk Road touched many different lands and cultures. But it probably had the greatest effect on the people of Central Asia. Without the Silk Road, this hard-to-reach region might have had very few visitors from the outside world. But because there were fortunes to be made by carrying goods through Central Asia, visitors did come through—lots of them. And not just traders.

words to know

ethnic group: people with common ancestors sharing customs, languages, and beliefs.

clan: groups of families that are related.

aksakal: a respected senior member of a tribe, from the Turkic word for "white beard."

The Silk Road brought adventurers, missionaries, and invading armies. Some passed through. Many stayed and became part of the community, or created new ones.

Central Asian cities grew rich catering to Silk Road travelers. Local craftsmakers added their products to the goods traded from East and West. As a result, Central Asia built connections with Greece, Rome, the Middle East, Persia, India, China, and beyond.

There are several main **ethnic groups** in Central Asia today. The Kazakhs, Kyrgyzs, Tajiks, Turkmen, and Uzbeks live in independent countries formed after the break-up of the Soviet Union in 1991. Pashtuns are the biggest group living in Afghanistan. Uighurs and Mongols live in autonomous regions in China.

Each ethnic group has its own identity, but scientific evidence shows that all the groups are closely related. We can see that in their cultures and their values.

Most speak one of the Turkic languages, which are related to Turkish, the language spoken in Turkey. People in Afghanistan and Tajikistan use a form of the Persian language spoken in Iran. Almost all follow Islam.

Family loyalty is an important trait. So is loyalty to their **clan** or tribe. Central Asian people have great respect for **aksakals** or "white beards," the senior members of their clan. And they honor and preserve their history and culture through storytelling.

Fascinating Fact

In some Central Asian tribes, members must be able to name seven generations of their family tree.

CENTRAL ASIAN STORYTELLING

In Central Asia there is a long tradition of storytellers who sing epic tales about national heroes. The *Epic of Manas* from Kyrgyzstan celebrated its thousandth anniversary in 1995. Noted for its poetry and exciting adventures, it tells the story of Manas, a hero with great supernatural strength. Manas fights off his people's enemies and brings his country together. Some versions of the epic run as long as half a million lines. It takes many years for a *Manas* storyteller, known as a *Manaschi*, to learn it all. This Kyrgyz epic is 20 times longer than the *Iliad* and the *Odyssey* combined. ✤

CITY LIFE AND NOMADIC LIFE

At the height of the Silk Road, the people who settled in its cities had very different lifestyles from the nomads who wandered across the nearby plains.

City people might work as shopkeepers or skilled workers providing supplies, food, and services. Craftspeople created carpets, saddles, leather goods, and metalwork. On the outskirts of the cities farmers grew fruits and vegetables and sold them in the markets to local families and to travelers.

Fascinating Fact

A typical nomad family unit used about 200 pounds (100 kilograms) of wool a year to make clothing and felt rugs.

Nomadic life revolved around caring for animals. As the seasons changed, nomads moved their homes to places where there was enough food and water for their herds. Depending on where they lived, nomads raised horses, sheep, goats, camels, oxen, or yaks. They used their animals for carrying loads, pulling carts, or for riding. The animals provided wool, milk, and meat. Their skins were used for leather, and their dung was dried and burned for fuel. The nomads were excellent horseback riders. And they were known for their ability to hunt or fight while riding, which made them fast and powerful on the attack.

CENTRAL ASIANS IN QUEENS, NEW YORK

Today a large community of people from Central Asia lives in Queens, New York, where they keep many of the traditions from the Silk Road alive. The Queens neighborhood of Rego Park—sometimes called Regostan—boasts Central Asian restaurants, carpet shops, musicians, and artists. The people in Rego Park are Jews from Bukhara. There are also communities of Kalmuks (Mongols) in Richmond, California, and New Jersey. ✣

Because nomads were often on the move, they couldn't grow or store extra food or make all the items they needed for their homes. Instead they traded with townspeople, exchanging animals or leather for grain, tools, or furnishings.

Relations between nomads and settlers were not always friendly. Sometimes, armed nomadic tribes on horseback swooped in on nearby cities. They would demand payment to leave the cities alone, or simply take what they wanted and flee. City dwellers rarely chased the raiders. They couldn't ride as fast or as long as nomadic horsemen. And they couldn't leave their homes and fields for long periods of time, either.

HOUSING

Although the lifestyles of townspeople and nomads were different in many ways, their homes had several elements in common. Usually their houses were plain on the outside, but richly decorated inside. Furniture consisted mainly of floor mats and cushions, a low table or stool, and trunks for storage. A common room was used for meals and for entertaining guests. If their homes were big enough, both settled people and nomads set aside separate areas for men and for women.

City houses had high walls surrounding a private inner courtyard. Typically the outside wall had no windows and just one entrance, making it secure and private. In the drier regions, buildings were often made of dried clay bricks covered in plaster.

In areas where more trees were available, buildings were made of wood and stone. Three generations of a family might live in one enclosure, with more than one house inside the courtyard walls. Sometimes animals were kept in a separate section of the courtyard.

Nomads usually lived at least part of the year in a large dome-shaped tent called a yurt or ger. A yurt consisted of a collapsible frame covered in large strips of felt. The wall frame was made of criss-crossing wooden slats, and the cone-shaped roof frame looked something like a wagon wheel with a hole in the middle. The door was usually a rolled-up piece of felt. Modern yurts often have a fancy, carved wooden door. Traditionally the doorway faced south toward the sun, to let in the most amount of light. A small yurt could be taken apart in under an hour and loaded on a camel or ox to be moved.

Inside, the yurt had a fire in the middle for heat and for cooking. The hole in the roof served as a chimney. Since the walls of the yurt were made of pieces of felt, they could be rolled up in hot weather to let in a breeze. Extra rugs could be hung for insulation when it was cold. Men and honored guests stayed on the west side with the saddles and tools. Women and children stayed on the east, with the bedding, rugs, cookware, and food. This was all according to custom based on religious and superstitious beliefs.

> ## Fascinating Fact
> During the Mongolian Empire, Marco Polo wrote of seeing large yurts on rolling platforms pulled by huge teams of oxen.

MAKE YOUR OWN
Model Yurt

This model yurt takes a few hours to build, but it has many realistic details. You can add a fancy wooden door if you like instead of the felt, roll-up kind.

---

1 To make the wall frame poles, cut the bamboo skewers into pieces 3 inches (7½ centimeters) long. Measure and mark the skewers with the pencil. Notch the wood at the marks with the scissors, then bend back and forth gently until the pieces separate. If you are using thin plastic stirrer straws, just cut each one in half. You will need a total of 76 poles.

2 Cut two pieces of tape 15 inches (38 centimeters) long. These will go along the top and bottom of the yurt walls. Lay them out horizontally, one above and one below, sticky side up. Leave a space of 2 inches (5 centimeters) in between.

3 Begin sticking the poles to the pieces of tape. Leave half the tape showing above the top and below the bottom of the poles. Starting with the bottom tape, place the bottom end of the first pole all the way to the left. Tilt the top of the pole about 1 inch (2 centimeters) to the right of the bottom end. Keep placing poles at the same angle, leaving about each ½ inch (1 centimeter) in between each one.

supplies

- 30 bamboo skewers or 40 thin plastic stirrer straws
- ruler
- pencil
- scissors
- thin masking tape (cut if too wide)
- skinny wood craft sticks
- glue
- string
- cardboard paper towel tube, or strip of thin cardboard
- gray or off-white felt
- craft sticks, cardboard, decorative ribbon, paint (optional)

4 Make a second strip of poles the same way. Flip the second strip over and place it on top of the first strip. The poles should criss-cross. Press the two strips of tape together to attach them securely. Trim any excess.

5 Cut craft sticks to make a door frame 3 inches high and 2 inches wide (7½ by 5 centimeters). Glue and let dry.

6 Stand up the criss-cross wall frame and bend it in a circle. Tie it to the door frame with the string. Use tape if needed.

7 For the roof opening, make a ring of cardboard about ¼ inch wide and 1½ inches across (½ by 4 centimeters) by cutting a section from a paper towel tube or bending a thin piece of cardboard to size and taping together. Tape four poles to the bottom edge of the ring, evenly spaced. Tape the other end of the poles to the walls of the yurt. The roof should have a cone shape. Tape three roof poles between each of the original roof poles, spacing them evenly.

8 For the covering cut 5 or 6 pieces of felt about 3 inches by 6 inches (7½ by 15 centimeters). Drape 3 or 4 over the roof, leaving the hole in the middle partly uncovered. Tie them down by laying some strings across them, attached to the wall at either end. Wrap 2 pieces of felt around the wall frame. Tie a piece of string onto the doorframe near the bottom, wrap around the wall, and secure on the other side of the doorframe. Do the same around the top of the wall. You can also use a piece of decorative ribbon tape to secure.

9 Cut a piece of felt 2 inches wide and 3 inches high (5 by 7½ centimeters) for the door. Roll it up and tie with a piece of string at either end. Attach to the top of the door opening with a piece of tape on the inside.

FOOD AND DRINK ALONG THE SILK ROAD

Food along the Silk Road is a blend of many different cultures.

- **Nan:** a type of flat bread also found in India.

- **Samsa:** a meat pie in a flaky crust, similar to an Indian samosa.

- **Shashlyk:** a Turkish dish similar to shish-kebab, with pieces of meat cooked on a **skewer** over an open flame.

- **Beshbarmak:** the national dish of the Kazahk and Kyrgyz people, made with horse meat, sausage, and noodles. The name means "five fingers," which is how it is supposed to be eaten.

- **Plov:** a rice dish similar to the Mediterranean rice pilaf, with meat and vegetables such as onions, carrots, raisins, and chickpeas cooked in a heavy pot called a *kazan*.

- **Manti:** a meat-filled dumpling larger than a Chinese wonton that can be steamed, fried, or boiled, and topped with yogurt. Nomads carried dried or frozen manti to boil when needed.

- **Lagman:** a noodle dish or soup made with fried **mutton**, peppers, onions, and tomatoes. In Central Asia it is considered the inspiration for Chinese lo mein noodles and Italian spaghetti.

- **Chai:** the name for tea, usually served with camel or goat milk, salt, and butter. ✢

words to know

skewer: a thin pointed stick for holding small pieces of food over a fire.

mutton: meat from an older sheep.

Central Asian Lagman Noodles

supplies

- ♂ large and small mixing bowls and spoon

- ♂ 3½ cups (800 milliliters) flour

- ♂ ½ teaspoon (2 milliliters) salt

- ♂ ½ cup (100 milliliters) water

- ♂ 1 egg

- ♂ 2 tablespoons (30 milliliters) oil

- ♂ flour-covered board and rolling pin

- ♂ knife or pizza cutter

- ♂ large pot of boiling water, salted

Lagman is similar to the egg noodles you can buy in the supermarket. Try them alone or with butter. For a more authentic Central Asian dinner, spoon some meat stew over the noodles. This recipe makes enough noodles for six people.

1 Mix flour and salt together in the large bowl. Pour the water into the small bowl. Add the egg and oil and stir briskly. Make an indentation in the flour. Pour in the liquid ingredients. Stir until everything is moist and starts to stick together into a ball of dough.

2 Pat some flour on your hands. Put the dough on the floured board and press into a flat ball. To knead, fold the dough towards you. Press down. Turn the dough one-quarter of the way around. Continue folding, pressing, and turning the dough for five minutes until it becomes smooth and stretchy. If too dry, add a few drops of water. If too sticky, sprinkle on a little more flour.

3 Press the dough flat. Use the rolling pin to roll the dough out into a very thin rectangle. If necessary cut the dough in half and roll out one half at a time.

4 Slice the dough into noodles about ¼ inch (½ centimeter) wide with the knife or pizza cutter. Let dry at least 2 hours. To cook, boil the noodles until done, just a couple of minutes.

CLOTHING

Traditional clothes in the Silk Road region revealed many aspects of a person's identity. Different groups often used their own colors, patterns, fabric, and embroidery. Clothes also indicated religion, age, and importance in society.

Women typically wore baggy pants and a long shirt. Their sleeves were very long, sometimes completely covering the hands. They often wore a coat or vest. In some areas women followed the Muslim custom of covering their faces with veils. In others, only their hair was covered with a scarf or shawl. Girls wore a type of colorful skullcap called a *tuppi* or *tokai*.

A man's traditional outfit was similar, except that a man's hat was pointy, like a cone. Important men sometimes wore a **turban**. Men wore high leather boots or moccasins on their feet.

Nomads often carried their wealth in the form of clothing and jewelry. Women covered themselves in gold or silver earrings, bracelets, pendants, and forehead or chest coverings. Men wore heavy rings that showed their power and position. They also carried ceremonial swords or daggers. Their horses wore decorated saddles and harnesses.

Fascinating Fact

Pants were invented in the Silk Road region to make it possible to sit comfortably on a horse.

70

HORSES AND WEAPONS

Horses and weapons were vital to the nomads who lived along the Silk Road. Nomads invented the **stirrup** and the **saddle**, and used them to conquer Asia. By sitting in the saddle and putting their feet in the stirrups, riders could control their horses with their legs. Meanwhile, they could use both hands to shoot with a bow and arrow.

words to know

turban: a long piece of fabric wrapped around the head that completely covers the hair.

stirrup: a footrest shaped like a loop used for horseback riding.

saddle: a seat for the rider of a horse.

The Mongols' saddle was made of wood and leather. It was rubbed with sheep's fat to soften it and make it more comfortable for horse and rider. Another important invention was the leather saddlebag. Riders used them to carry water, cooking pots, and preserved food. Saddlebags made it possible for the riders to stay out for long periods of time.

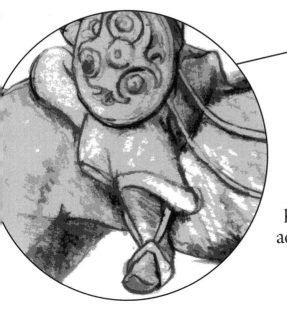

The Mongols also had a special bow made from layers of wood and horn. It could shoot an arrow more than 1,000 feet (300 meters). One Chinese writer said the Mongols "took possession of the world through this advantage of bow and horse."

71

GAMES AND SPORTS

Popular sports in Central Asia include wrestling and falconry. But the most unusual—and most gruesome—is a game from Afghanistan called *buzkashi*. The game is played on horseback, like polo. But instead of hitting a small ball with a long-handled mallet, *buzkashi* players try to grab a dead goat and carry it to the other end of the field. Pushing and shoving are part of the game, and broken bones are common. In the time of Genghis Khan, it is said the body of a dead enemy was used instead of a dead animal. Today *buzkashi* is played during holidays and special occasions such as weddings.

PROTECTING YOUNG RIDERS

Even today, many Mongol children learn to ride a horse before they can walk. During the springtime festival of Naadam, boys and girls as young as four or five take part in traditional horse races. Hundreds of horses race at once, at speeds of up to 50 miles per hour. More than 30,000 children compete in horse races each year.

But some lawmakers and international groups believe children's horse races have gotten more dangerous. Races are now held year-round, even in below-freezing winter weather. And although riders are supposed to wear pads and helmets, many do not. Rules that say children must be at least seven years old to race are ignored. To help young riders, some groups have started giving away special riding helmets to children before the start of big races. ✧

Indoors, children in Mongolia like to play a game known as **shagai**. These are the ankle bones of sheep and were probably an early form of dice. In English, they are sometimes called "shooting bones." When tossed, *shagai* have four sides they can land on. The sides are called "sheep," "goat," "camel," and "horse." The other two sides are rounded, so the bones don't stay in those positions.

There are many different *shagai* games. In some games the pieces are flicked with the fingers, as in the game of marbles. Other games involve tossing the pieces up in the air and picking up certain ones while leaving others alone, like in the game of jacks.

words to know

falconry: using trained falcons to hunt other small birds.

polo: a team game played on horseback by hitting a ball with a long-handled mallet.

shagai: an early form of playing dice made from the bones of a sheep.

LEARN TO PLAY A
Shagai Shooting Bones Dice Game

Finding sheep ankle bones to play *shagai* with may be difficult. But one game you can try, using dice instead of sheep bones, is called "Horse Race."

1 Use the markers to set up a racecourse.

2 Each player gets a die. These are the race horses.

3 Taking turns, the players move around the racecourse by flicking or shooting their pieces with their fingers.

4 Whoever reaches the end of the racecourse first, wins.

chapter 5

Cities and Towns
Along the Silk Road

Many cities along the Silk Road got their start as small oasis towns. In places where caravans stopped to rest and re-supply, markets grew. Tradespeople opened shops. Missionaries and religious leaders built temples and mosques. Rulers used the taxes and fees they collected from travelers to pay for palaces and monuments to their glory. All this activity helped turn a small rest stop into a busy **metropolis**.

But when traffic on the Silk Road ended, not every city survived. In some places today, visitors can still see magnificent structures built centuries before. In others, historic ruins and museums are all that are left to show where great cities once thrived.

MARKETS AND BAZAARS

The first markets developed where people produced more food, tools, or other supplies than they needed. A person would offer something another person wanted, and get something they wanted back in return. For instance, a rug merchant would trade carpets for melons. This type of trade is called **barter**.

As trade developed, people started using gold, jewels, silk, or even spices as payment. Eventually bags of gold and bolts of silk were replaced by coins and paper money. These were much easier to carry, and much easier to trade. Paper money took a while to catch on, however.

> ## words to know
>
> **metropolis:** an important city.
>
> **barter:** to trade by exchanging one kind of good for another.
>
> **bazaar:** a market made up of rows of shops or stalls, sometimes specializing in one thing.

The first traders were employed by rulers who kept the profits themselves. But eventually traders starting working on their own. When traders stopped at oasis towns, they would lay out their wares along the side of the road to trade. This informal trading led to regular marketplaces in specific places at specific times. When markets got too big, they were divided up into separate **bazaars**. Each bazaar specialized in different kinds of goods.

supplies

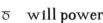

- money
- item you'd like to buy
- will power

In a Silk Road market, bargaining over price is a tradition. Experienced buyers pride themselves on paying as little as possible. Meanwhile, sellers want their customers to think they've gotten a good deal—while still making a nice profit. Learn the rules of bargaining and you can save money at garage sales or flea markets.

1 Research the item you want to buy. Is the best too expensive? Are there other good choices? If the item is used, what kind of wear and tear is OK, and what could cause problems?

2 When you figure out how much the item usually costs, decide how much it's worth to you. What do you think is fair and what's the most you're willing to spend? How much money do you have, and how much will you use or enjoy the item? Keep these numbers in mind, but don't tell the seller!

3 Don't buy the first item you see. Take some time to compare what other sellers have. Look them over and get as much information from each seller as you can.

4 Once you've found the one you want, ask what it costs. If the price is much too high, say so and wait to see if the seller asks how much you were thinking of paying.

5 Here's where the fun starts. Offer your fair price—or lower—and see if that's acceptable. If it's not, the seller will probably name another price.

6 If the new price is acceptable, take it, or make a counter-offer. If it's still way too high, say thanks and walk away.

7 Don't walk too fast, though. When the seller sees you're ready to leave, you may get one last deal. If not, don't worry, with enough time and patience, you'll usually find what you want at what you're willing to pay.

THE ABACUS ON THE SILK ROAD

The **abacus** is a tool for adding up numbers quickly. It was used by merchants and traders all along the Silk Road. First developed in the Mediterranean, its name means "dust," because the idea for the abacus came from making marks in the sand. The Greeks and Romans used an early version. It had a board with grooves and loose balls that could be rolled back and forth.

words to know

abacus: a tool for adding and subtracting using beads on rods.

irrigation: a system for bringing water through ditches to farmland.

minaret: a high tower used to call Muslims to prayer five times a day.

madrassa: a Muslim religious school or college.

When the abacus arrived in China over the Silk Road, the Chinese improved it even more. Instead of balls, they used beads that could slide up and down on rods so they wouldn't get lost. A center bar across the frame of the abacus divided the rods into "heaven" and "earth." Each rod had two "heaven beads" above the center bar and five "earth beads" below. This type of abacus is still sometimes used in Chinese schools and shops today.

SILK ROAD CITIES IN CENTRAL ASIA

Central Asian cities grew and prospered along the Silk Road for centuries under many different empires. But rulers from Genghis Khan to Timur changed the landscape throughout the region. Their armies destroyed many cities. Some cities never recovered. Others were rebuilt by their conquerors, who added their own grand monuments.

Samarkand, Uzbekistan: When Alexander the Great conquered Samarkand in 329 BCE, he said "Everything I have heard about the beauty of the city is indeed true except that it is much more beautiful than I imagined." At the time, Samarkand was a green and pleasant city kept watered by **irrigation** canals. Because of its location at the crossroads of China, India, and Persia, Samarkand became a major center for crafts and trade.

Genghis Khan destroyed the city in 1220 CE, but in 1370 Timur rebuilt it and made it his capital. It soon became famous for culture and learning. In 1720, an earthquake drove away all the inhabitants. It took 50 years for new settlers to bring the city back to life.

> **Fascinating Fact**
>
> The Kalyan Minaret was also known as the Tower of Death, because criminals were executed by being thrown from it.

Bukhara, Uzbekistan: Bukhara has been called the best-preserved medieval city in Central Asia. Part of the Persian Empire, it is filled with beautiful buildings like the Kalyan **Minaret**. Constructed in 1127 CE, the minaret is 150 feet (45 meters) high and can be seen throughout the whole city. It's known for the decorative patterns of its bricks. Genghis Khan destroyed the city in 1220 but ordered his troops to leave the tower alone. After becoming the capital, Bukhara grew and was soon home to more than 100 **madrassas** and 300 mosques.

MAKE YOUR OWN
Abacus

Learning to use the abacus takes time and practice. You can make your own and try counting on it.

Supplies

- 9 craft sticks
- glue
- pencil
- ruler
- 5 bamboo skewers cut to 4–6 inches (10–15 centimeters) long
- scissors
- 35 pony beads big enough to slide on the skewers

1 Glue two craft sticks together, one on top of the other. Make two more double craft sticks the same way. Let dry.

2 Take another craft stick and lay it out horizontally. Make a pencil mark in the center. Make two more marks a little way in from the ends. Then make two more marks centered between the other marks.

3 Put glue along the pencil lines and lay the lower ends of the skewers along them. Put a dot of glue on top of each skewer and lay one of the double craft sticks on top. Let dry.

4 Slide five "earth" beads on each skewer. Two thirds of the way from the lower end of the skewers, glue another craft stick under the skewers, parallel to the bottom bar, to make the center bar. Put dots of glue on top of the skewers and lay another one of the double craft sticks on top. Make sure the beads don't touch the wet glue. Let dry.

5 Slide two "heaven" beads on each skewer. Glue another craft stick under the upper end of the skewers to make the top bar. Put dots of glue on the skewers and lay the third set of double craft sticks on top. When dry, flip the abacus over so the double sticks are on the bottom.

HOW TO USE THE ABACUS

The abacus uses rods in place of the ones column, tens column, and so on used in written math. On each rod, the earth beads below the center bar are each worth 1, and the heaven beads above the bar are worth 5. To count a bead, you push it towards the center bar. When no beads are pushed toward the center bar, that rod shows 0. To start counting, "zero out" the abacus by pushing all the beads away from the center bar. Push one earth bead up. That's 1. Push one more up to show 2, another to show 3, and so on until you have all five earth beads at the center bar to show 5.

Now, to show 6, push four earth beads down so only one earth bead is still at the center bar. Then push one heaven bead down towards the center bar. You should have one earth bead (worth 1) and one heaven bead (worth 5) for a total value of 6.

Hundreds Column

Tens Column

Ones Column

Do the same thing to show numbers on the tens rod, the hundreds rod, etc. For instance, push one earth bead up to show 10, two earth beads to show 20. How would you show 537? (Answer: five earth beads on the hundreds rod, three earth beads on the tens rod, and two earth beads and one heaven bead on the ones rod.) ✛

Bactria (Balkh), Afghanistan: The village called Balkh today was once known as Bactria, the center of the mighty Bactrian Empire. The Arabs called it the "Mother of Cities." In 330 BCE Alexander the Great made it his eastern capital. It became a major center of learning. The city's importance grew even more when it became the junction of the eastern and western portions of the Silk Road. Bactria was also destroyed by the Mongols in 1220 CE. Fifty years later Marco Polo reported that the city was still in ruins. Today all that remains are the mud-brick walls around its border and a ruined mosque on the outskirts.

Bamiyan, Afghanistan: In the sixth century CE, Bamiyan was a major destination for Buddhist pilgrims. Its main attractions were two giant Buddha statues. The taller of the two was 180 feet (55 meters) tall, or about the height of an 18-story building. The statues were carved out of the soft rock of the cliffs surrounding the city. The stone was plastered over and covered with gold. Sadly, the statutes became famous in 2001 after they were blown up with dynamite by the Taliban, a group of Muslim extremists, which then controlled Afghanistan.

CARAVANSERAI

When weary travelers on the Silk Road arrived in an oasis city, they would head for the local **caravanserai**. A *caravanserai* was an inn where traders could stay for many days. They could relax, rest up, and compare stories with traders from other lands. In the thirteenth century, the Seljuk Empire in Turkey and Persia built a system of *caravanserais* throughout the empire. They offered three days of free food and lodging. They even included free medical care!

The typical *caravanserai* was a stone building with an inner courtyard. The entrance was large enough for a loaded camel to pass through. The courtyard often contained baths, dining areas, storerooms, and treasuries for securing valuables. There were shops and sometimes markets. Stables were provided for the camels. For the travelers, the bedrooms had built-in fireplaces, shelves, and sleeping platforms. They were often decorated with traditional Islamic **geometric** designs. More importantly, the *caravanserais* had iron doors and guard towers for protection from thieves and raiders. ✦

words to know

caravanserai: an inn providing services and shelter for caravans.

geometric: a style of art that uses simple shapes such as lines, circles, and squares.

SILK ROAD CITIES IN CHINA

The Silk Road cities of western China have many ties to Central Asia. They share language, religion, history and culture with Central Asian countries that sets them apart from the rest of China. But the Silk Road also brought outsiders into the heart of China. And that influence can still be seen today.

Loulan, Xinjiang Uighur Autonomous Region: Founded in 176 BCE, Loulan was a major stop on the Silk Road. But around 630 CE sandstorms covered the region, rivers disappeared, and the city was swallowed by the desert. Archaeologists exploring the ruins have found more than 200 naturally preserved **mummies**. The oldest date back before the time of the Silk Road, about 3,800 years ago. One is a woman with long, reddish hair and plaid clothing known as the Loulan Beauty. Scientific tests have traced these mysterious mummies back to Europe. Nobody knows how they came to live in the heart of Asia.

> ## words to know
>
> **mummy:** a body that has been preserved so that it doesn't decay.
>
> **sutra:** a teaching of Buddha making up part of Buddhist holy writings.
>
> **pagoda:** a Buddhist temple, or place of worship, with an upward curving roof.

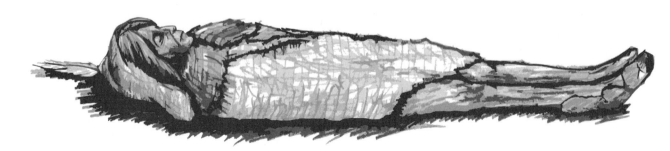

Dunhuang: As the main entryway from Central Asia where the northern and southern Silk Roads met, Dunhuang was important for trade and security. During periods of Chinese control they built defenses to block attacks from the west. Buddhist monks coming from India stopped here to learn Chinese before continuing on. As a result, Dunhuang became a center for translating Buddhist **sutras** into Chinese.

Not far from Dunhuang are the Magao Caves, or Caves of a Thousand Buddhas. These are 492 man-made caves, dating from the fourth to the fourteenth centuries CE. The caves are richly decorated with religious wall paintings, statues, and other works of art. After being abandoned for centuries, the caves were made famous in the twentieth century by the explorer Marc Aurel Stein. Among the 40,000 scrolls he discovered was the oldest known complete printed book, the Diamond Sutra. It bears a date of 868 CE.

Chang'an (Xi'an): Built in 194 BCE, Chang'an was the Chinese endpoint of the Silk Road during much of the route's history. The city was China's capital during the Han and Tang dynasties. At times it was the largest city in the world. Many foreign princes, merchants, religious pilgrims, and traveling entertainers made their home here. The city once had Zoroastrian, Nestorian Christian, Muslim, Jewish, and Buddhist churches, temples, and **pagodas**.

85

KUBLAI KHAN'S SUMMER CAPITAL

In the 1250s CE, Kublai Khan built a spectacular summer palace at Shangdu (now Duolun in the Mongol Autonomous Region of China). The palace was large enough to hold 6,000 people. Its walls were of gold and silver fastened with 200 silk cords, so it could be taken apart and moved. Marco Polo's description made the palace famous in Europe, where it was called "Xanadu." Today only ruins remain, but the English poet Samuel Coleridge wrote a famous poem about the palace in 1816, which began:

> *In Xanadu did Kublai Khan*
> *A stately pleasure-dome decree:*
> *Where Alph, the sacred river, ran*
> *Through caverns measureless to man*
> *Down to a sunless sea.* ✛

The famous Bell Tower and Drum Tower of Chang'an were built in the 1300s CE. The bell sounded in the morning and the drum at night to signal the opening and closing of the city gates.

Today Chang'an is called Xi'an, and is best known for the Terracotta Army. The Army consists of more than 7,000 clay statues of soldiers and horses. Each life-size statue has its own unique face and armor. The statues were buried with Emperor Shi Huangdi around 210 BCE. Archaeologists discovered the tomb in 1974, and are still studying it today.

chapter 6
The Spread of Ideas, Technology, and Traditions

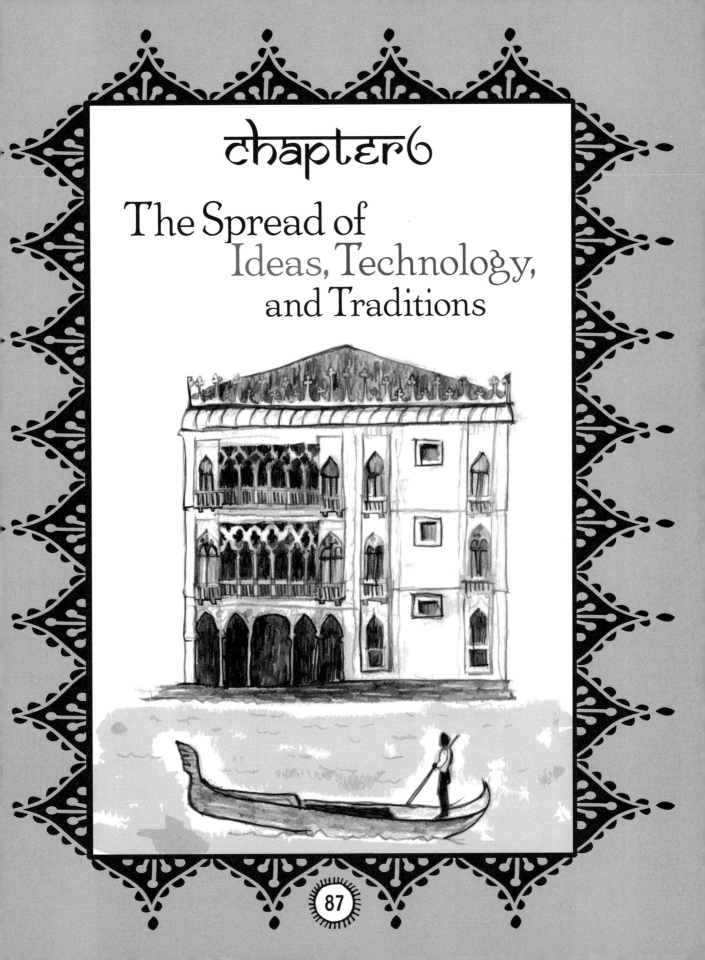

Fascinating Fact

The first printed version of the Quran, the holy book of Islam, was published in Venice, Italy, in 1538. It was created for sale to Muslim countries. But because the publishers didn't speak Arabic, it was filled with mistakes.

Something just as important as merchandise was also carried along the Silk Road: ideas. As travelers journeyed along the various trade routes, they encountered many new things—new languages, inventions, religions, and art and entertainment. It is the ideas, even more than the trade goods, which truly shaped and changed the places the Silk Road touched.

LANGUAGES

Learning languages was one way people along the Silk Road shared foreign cultures. And there were a lot of different languages to learn. Ancient documents found in Buddhist caves near the Silk Road were written in more than 20 different languages.

Some of the most commonly used Silk Road languages were Turkic, Chinese, Persian, Arabic, and Indian. Other languages included Greek, Latin, Hebrew, Russian, and Mongolian. Silk Road guides usually did double duty as translators. Merchants often knew how far they had traveled by counting the number of interpreters it took to get from one point to another.

words to know

Quran: holy book of Islam.

LEARN WORDS WITH
Trade Route
Origins

You probably know some words from the Silk Road region without even realizing it. Many English words originated somewhere along the various trade routes. Can you hear the foreign roots of these English words?

Turkish

yogurt: *a fermented dairy product.*

Chinese

ketchup: *from ke tziap, a type of fish sauce.*

typhoon: *from tai meaning "great" and feng meaning "wind," a great windstorm.*

Persian

balcony: *from balaa meaning "above" and khana meaning "house."*

candy: *from qand, meaning "sugar."*

magic: *from magus, meaning "sorcerer."*

pajama: *from pa meaning "leg" and jama meaning "clothing."*

Arabic

algebra: *from al-jabr, meaning "the restoring of missing parts," a type of math.*

ghoul: *from ghul, meaning "evil spirit."*

jar: *from jarrah, meaning "a clay container."*

Indian

orange: *from Sanskrit naranga meaning "orange tree."*

shampoo: *from Hindi and Urdu capo, meaning "rub."*

89

MONEY

Although bartering was the main form of payment on the Silk Road, money got its start in this part of the world as well. The Chinese made the earliest known coins around 1000 BCE. They were cast from bronze and copper and looked like seashells, which were an earlier form of money. Next came round coins with holes so the coins could be kept on a string. Outside of China, round coins bearing portraits of gods and emperors began to appear in modern-day Turkey around 500 BCE. The idea soon spread to Greece, Persia, and Rome, where they made coins from precious metals such as silver and gold.

Fascinating Fact

By 1455 CE, the Chinese had issued so many bills that they weren't worth the paper they were printed on. The country went back to coins and didn't use paper money again for several centuries.

The idea of paper money may have come from a system used by Muslim traders called *hawala*, which means "trust" in Arabic. It was designed to protect traders from being robbed along the route. Instead of paying the seller, the buyer would deposit money in a safer location. Then the buyer would give the seller a code word that would permit the seller to pick up the money.

THE SPREAD OF PAPER MONEY

Marco Polo was very impressed by the idea of paper money, which was unknown in Europe. He described how Kublai Khan ordered "all merchants arriving from India or other countries, and bringing with them gold or silver or gems and pearls" to exchange them for bills. Even though they were just pieces of paper made from mulberry tree bark, he wrote,

"All these pieces of paper are issued with as much solemnity
and authority as, if they were of pure gold or silver;
and on every piece a variety of officials, whose duty it is,
have to write their names, and to put their seals . . .
[T]he money is then authentic.
Anyone forging it would be punished with death." ✛

In 806 CE the Chinese began using a similar system called *fei qian*, or "flying cash." Instead of a code word, they gave sellers paper money certificates. This led to paper bills around 1000 CE.

INVENTIONS

Many of the ideas and inventions that traveled along the Silk Road were so powerful that they literally changed the course of history. The stirrup allowed the Mongols to take over a continent. Money made it easier to buy and sell goods. Not every invention had an immediate effect, but many became very important as time went on.

Paper: Few inventions had as lasting an effect as the Chinese invention of paper around 100 CE. Before paper, the Chinese used rolls of silk or thin strips of bamboo. In Europe people used **parchment** made from animal skins. In the Middle East they used **papyrus**, made from a special plant that only grew in Egypt. And in India they used palm leaves.

These materials were time consuming to make. Parchment was expensive, papyrus was not very strong, and silk was difficult to use. Paper, on the other hand, was cheap, sturdy, easy to make in large amounts, and easy to handle. It could be made from tree bark or rags woven from plant fibers.

Papermaking did not spread immediately. Perhaps the Chinese kept the process a secret, just as they did with silkmaking. But, by the fourth century CE, merchants from Central Asia were sending letters home written on paper. And by 793 CE, a papermaking industry had developed in Baghdad. But in Europe paper wasn't widely used until about 1150 CE.

> # words to know
>
> **parchment:** writing material made from specially prepared animal skin.
>
> **papyrus:** writing material made from strips of the papyrus plant.
>
> **scribe:** a person who copies writings by hand.
>
> **printing press:** a machine that presses inked type onto paper.

Printing: Printing began sometime between the fourth and seventh centuries CE. At first, characters were printed using hand-carved wooden blocks that were stamped on paper.

Then movable type was invented by a Chinese craftsman named Bi Sheng around 1041 CE. It used individually carved, reusable characters made of hardened clay.

Buddhists helped spread printing to other parts of the Silk Road. The small, printed, religious booklets they carried were good luck charms. Many of these were found in the caves at Dunhuang along with the Diamond Sutra.

Around the time of Marco Polo, Silk Road travelers brought the idea of printing to Europe. At first, Italians made books using hand-carved blocks. Then, in 1456, Johannes Gutenberg came up with his own movable type machine, the **printing press**. Gutenberg's invention changed the history of Europe by making books cheap enough for ordinary people to own. This gave them power through knowledge and information they never had before.

> ## Fascinating Fact
>
> Many different versions of Marco Polo's book exist because the **scribes** who made hand-written copies of it changed things, either by accident or on purpose.

93

MAKE YOUR OWN
Paper

The technique the Chinese came up with for making paper is the same method used today. Plant material is soaked until it is soft, then chopped up into a pulp and spread out to dry in a single sheet. Here's a very quick and easy way to make recycled paper using old newspapers instead of raw plant material. You'll need to do it outside or near a sink. And when making the pulp, don't use containers or utensils that are used for eating.

supplies

- scrap paper pieces from a shredder or small torn-up pieces of paper
- wide-mouth jar, about 1 quart (1 liter)
- spoon or stick
- hot water
- 3 tablespoons (45 milliliters) cornstarch
- aluminum pie pan, or plastic or foam plate
- aluminum foil
- sharp pencil
- waxed paper
- newspaper
- old towels or clean, absorbent rags

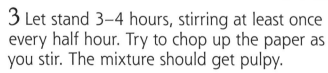

1 Fill the jar one-third to one-half full with paper pieces.

2 Add enough hot water to cover the paper. Stir.

3 Let stand 3–4 hours, stirring at least once every half hour. Try to chop up the paper as you stir. The mixture should get pulpy.

4 When the paper mixture is as smooth as you can get it, add the cornstarch. This will thicken it. Mix thoroughly.

5 Make a strainer by covering the pie pan tightly with the foil. Punch some small holes in the foil with the pencil.

6 Pour a thin layer of paper mixture onto the strainer. Carefully drain off excess water by tilting the plate back and forth. Fold up one side of the foil to make a little lip if needed to keep the paper mixture from running off the plate.

7 Cover the paper pulp with a piece of waxed paper. Press flat. Drain off more water if needed. Pull the foil away from the pie plate.

8 Turn the foil-waxed paper "sandwich" over so the waxed paper is on the bottom. Carefully lift off the foil so the paper pulp is on the waxed paper in a sheet.

9 Carefully lift the waxed paper with the mixture onto a flat surface covered with newspaper. Cover with a towel and press out more moisture. Flatten as you go. It should make a nice thin sheet.

10 When the paper is as dry as you can get it, set it in a warm spot for a few hours or overnight to dry completely.

Gunpowder: The Chinese invented gunpowder around 850 CE. Gunpowder was first used to make an **elixir** that was supposed to bring everlasting life. It took another hundred years before the Chinese found a military use for it. In the 1100s, they made the first cannons out of large bamboo tubes. The first known guns with metal barrels were made in 1290. Genghis Khan's armies used cannons against the Persians and Arabs.

By the 1300s, both Arabs and Europeans had improved the weapons and were using guns and cannons in warfare. In 1510 the Chinese hired Europeans to help them update their own inventions.

SCIENCE

Scientific knowledge—and some **pseudoscience**—also traveled along the Silk Road. Alexander the Great brought advances in medicine from India to Europe. Buddhist missionaries carried them to China. During the Middle Ages, the center of scientific learning was the Middle East. Jewish and Muslim traders helped spread this knowledge to both Europe and China.

words to know

elixir: a liquid with magical properties.

pseudoscience: false science.

astronomy: the study of objects in space.

navigation: finding directions for traveling using stars, maps, landmarks, or other methods.

astrolabe: an instrument for finding the position of objects in the sky for navigation.

astrology: an ancient science that tries to use objects in the sky to tell the future.

zodiac: sets of stars in the sky used for astrology.

Alchemy: Alchemy was a pseudoscience that became the basis of modern chemistry. It was practiced all along the Silk Road, from ancient Egypt and Greece to Persia, India, and China. In Europe it was popular into the eighteenth century CE. The goal of alchemy was to make elixirs that could turn common metals into gold or bring everlasting life. Alchemists built the first laboratories and did the first chemistry experiments. Their discoveries were later used to make colorful dyes, glass, and other products.

Astronomy and Astrology: Astronomy is the study of the sun, moon, and stars. It was used for navigation and to measure time and the seasons. The Mongols employed Muslim scholars who introduced tools such as the astrolabe and the globe. Under Timur, astronomers created a hand-drawn map of over 1,000 stars. It became a standard for Europe and China as well.

Astrology, or telling the future using the stars, is a pseudoscience that originated in the Middle East. It spread from there to Europe and then to Central Asia with Alexander the Great. Buddhist missionaries brought it with them to China. The Chinese eventually created their own version of the Western signs of the zodiac.

Medicine: The Indians developed a detailed knowledge of the human body, which they recorded in a book called the *Ayurveda* about 700 BCE. The Greeks picked up many ideas about the treatment of diseases from the Indians. Alexander the Great used Indian doctors to help treat venomous snakebites.

Knowledge of Indian medicine spread with Buddhism to China. The Buddhist caves in Dunhuang contained ancient medical writings in many different languages. One scroll from around 803 CE describes 10 **contagious** diseases of the time. Another scroll was called *Master Ling Yang's Secret Remedies.* It provided **incantations** used to summon devils and spirits to help with cures. There was even a cure for baldness, which told the patient to "rub in horse-mane oil regularly; the hair then begins to grow spontaneously."

Kublai Khan brought Muslim and Chinese doctors together to produce a guide containing all their medical knowledge. He also built a hospital in Khanbaliq for Chinese soldiers and officials.

THE BLACK DEATH

Diseases also passed along the Silk Road. One of the most deadly was the Black Death, also known as bubonic **plague**. The Black Death may have started in Central Asia. Gravestones uncovered in the Lake Issyk Kul area show that many people died from the plague there around 1338 CE. It spread quickly and killed two thirds of the people who became infected with it. The Black Death eventually killed tens of millions of people in both Europe and Asia. ✛

words to know

plague: a highly contagious and deadly disease.

contagious: easy to catch.

incantation: a magic spell.

halo: a circle of light around the head of a holy figure.

architect: an artist who designs buildings.

SILK ROAD ART

Up and down the Silk Road, artists were inspired by the styles and images from other countries. In the cities conquered by Alexander the Great, Buddhist monks began making their statues more like the life-like sculpture of the Greeks. Chinese landscape painters adapted the brightly colored, highly detailed style they saw in Persian miniature paintings. And European painters borrowed ideas like the **halo** from images in Buddhist temples to use in religious artwork.

Under Mongol rule, the spread of art styles became an official policy. When the Mongols captured a city, they took its artists, **architects,** and craftspeople prisoner. They moved these prisoners to other parts of their empire to rebuild and expand the cities they had destroyed. As a result, the cities of the Mongol empire reflected a broad range of styles from throughout the region.

Fascinating Fact

The golden halos that appear around the heads of saints in European paintings look a lot like round decorated brass trays from Egypt and Syria.

When Islam came to the Silk Road region, it brought its own style. Because Islam forbids the worship of idols, most Islamic art avoids showing humans or animals. There were few paintings and sculptures. Instead, Islamic art consists mainly of architecture, **calligraphy**, and handicrafts.

Islamic books and buildings are often decorated with scrolls, flowers, and geometric designs. When the Silk Road was at its height, many European architects used Islamic ideas in their own buildings. The geometric window grills of St. Mark's Basilica in Venice were probably copied from the Great Mosque in Damascus, Syria.

words to know

calligraphy: the art of beautiful writing.

exotic: different and exciting.

motif: an idea, pattern, image, or theme that is used in many works of art.

synagogue: a Jewish house of worship.

roof boss: a carved knob that covers where ribs on a ceiling come together.

European painters also liked including Islamic elements. They painted scenes of people surrounded by dishes, curtains, clothing, and rugs from the Silk Road region. The objects gave the work an **exotic** feel. Since these imported goods were so expensive, they showed that the person in the painting was wealthy and important. Some artists even painted fake Arabic writing on a piece of clothing or furniture in a scene so viewers would know it was set in the Middle East.

Art Motifs: It can be fun to trace a **motif** as it spreads from one end of the Silk Road to the other. For instance, the Persians put traditional Chinese lotus blossoms and clouds into their rug designs. And Chinese sculptors used Greek grapevines on buildings and ceramics.

One mysterious but widely seen motif is called The Three Hares. It consists of three rabbits running in a circle with their ears touching to make a triangle in the center. Although it looks like each rabbit has two ears, there are really only three ears altogether.

The oldest known Three Hares image was painted on the ceiling in one of the Caves of a Thousand Buddhas near Dunhuang, China. The image has also been found on a Persian copper coin, Mongol metal work, and in a Jewish **synagogue** in Germany. Dozens of Three Hares images can still be seen on **roof bosses** in churches in France, Germany, and England.

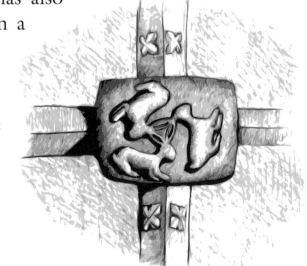

DRAW YOUR OWN
Interlocking
Design

The repeating geometric designs found in Islamic art and architecture followed patterns that mathematicians are just beginning to unravel today. You can make your own repeating Islamic-style patterns using only a few simple shapes: squares, triangles, six-sided hexagons, and stars. But to make them all fit together, you'll have to base them all on the same size unit—in this case, a circle.

1 Start by tracing around the can or glass on the cardboard. Make 3 circles and cut them out. Set one aside.

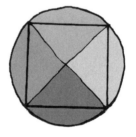
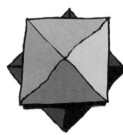

2 Take one circle and fold it in half. Then fold it in half again. Open it up and mark where the folds touch the edge of the circle. Use the ruler to connect these points with straight lines. Cut along the lines to make a square.

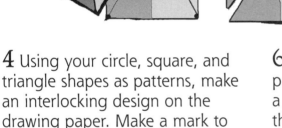

3 Make another square. Fold it in half so it becomes a rectangle. Open it up. Take the first square and place one side so its corners touch one bottom corner and the middle fold. Mark that spot. Use the ruler to make diagonal lines from that mark to the bottom two corners. Cut out your triangle.

4 Using your circle, square, and triangle shapes as patterns, make an interlocking design on the drawing paper. Make a mark to show the center. Then build your design outward from the center, making it even all around.

5 To make a six-pointed star, draw a triangle, flip the pattern upside down, slide it down a bit, and draw another triangle over it. Make a ring of connecting six-pointed stars to create a hexagon in between.

6 To make an eight-pointed star, draw a square. Turn the square pattern so the corners are in the middle of each side of the first square, and draw another square on top of it.

7 Can you figure out other ways to make triangles, stars, and other shapes that still fit together?

SCULPT YOUR OWN
Three Hares
"Roof Boss"

Three Hares sculptures come in all styles and materials. Here are directions for making modeling dough and creating a three-dimensional replica of a Three Hares roof boss. Tint the modeling material with food coloring, or paint when dry. **NOTE: An adult should be on hand to help cook the modeling dough.**

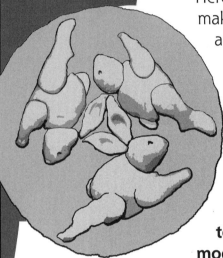

supplies

- ᴆ medium cooking pot
- ᴆ cooking spoon
- ᴆ 1 cup (250 milliliters) baking soda
- ᴆ ½ cup (125 milliliters) cornstarch
- ᴆ ¾ cup (175 milliliters) water
- ᴆ stove
- ᴆ wooden board
- ᴆ paper plate or round piece of cardboard for base
- ᴆ pen or pencil
- ᴆ food coloring or paint (optional)

1 Mix the baking soda and cornstarch in a pot. Add water and stir until smooth. Cook over low heat and stir until mixture becomes solid. Remove from the pot and allow to cool.

2 Knead the modeling dough on a wooden board by folding and pressing until smooth.

3 Mark the center of the plate or cardboard base. Model a triangle of rabbits' ears with the dough. The center mark goes in the middle of the triangle.

4 Make the first rabbit, except for the ears. Attach to one corner of the ear triangle. The ears should be attached to the back of the rabbit's head. If pieces of modeling dough don't stick together, put some water on your finger and wet them. If they fall apart after they dry, you can use glue to re-attach them.

MUSIC AND ENTERTAINMENT

Musicians and other entertainers also set out on the Silk Road in search of new audiences. And they brought new instruments with them. The violin or fiddle spread from the Middle East to Europe during the Crusades. From there Silk Road travelers introduced it throughout Central Asia and China.

Many different types of fiddles developed. One was called the *kemancheh*. It featured a small round wooden body covered in animal skin. The *kemancheh* rested on a spike sticking out the bottom, and was twisted back and forth so the bow could touch the right string. Another violin relative, the horse fiddle from Mongolia, had only two strings. Its neck was topped with a carving of a horse's head, and the pegs for tightening the two strings were called the horse's "ears."

Actors, dancers, and other performers were also popular along the Silk Road. In 108 BCE, the Han Emperor Wudi held a banquet for some foreign guests. According to Chinese history books, he brought in wrestlers, wild animal acts, and acrobats from Persia to entertain them. The records show that they presented tricks such as knife swallowing and fire spitting.

Fascinating Fact

The *kemancheh* is used in performances of the *maqom*, a long, complex piece. The *maqom* is **improvised**, and a performance can go on for several hours. It was the specialty of Bukharan Jewish musicians and singers, who even played for Muslim rulers.

Acrobats soon became a favorite form of entertainment for the Chinese. They even appeared in stone carvings and tomb paintings. The artwork showed them doing handstands, climbing poles, walking on tightropes, and juggling swords. When the Mongol ruler Kublai Khan built his palace at Khanbaliq, he included a theater where actors and performers from around the empire could perform.

LITERATURE, STORIES, AND MYTHS

Like other forms of art, stories were passed along the Silk Road and adapted to different places. *Cinderella* is an example of a story that spread throughout the entire Silk Road region. Each version contains different details, but they all tell about a girl who is treated badly when her mother dies and her father remarries. The girl usually has a magical helper who watches over her, and an item of clothing that reveals who she really is.

Fascinating Fact

Aesop's Fables is a well-known collection of animal stories from ancient Greece. It shares many of its plots with another collection from India about Buddha. Both feature stories where animals behave like humans to illustrate a wise saying or **moral**. Experts have not decided which version came first.

The earliest written version of the story of Cinderella comes from China about 850 CE. It is about a girl named Yeh-Shen. Instead of a fairy godmother, Yeh-Shen is helped by a magical fish. Her special shoe is golden, not glass, but it still helps unite her with the prince who wants to marry her. There are at least 300 other variations from places like Persia, Italy, Greece, and the Middle East.

words to know

improvise: to make up a piece of music while playing it.

moral: a valuable lesson to help people know how to behave.

MAKE YOUR OWN
Devil Sticks for Juggling

supplies

- ♂ scissors

- ♂ 3–4 old rubber bicycle tubes

- ♂ 2 wooden dowels about ¹/₂ inch (1¹/₂ centimeters) wide and 20 inches (50 centimeters) long

- ♂ 1 wooden dowel ¹/₂ inch (1¹/₂ centimeters) wide and 24 inches (60 centimeters) long

- ♂ electrical tape, any colors

- ♂ felt

Devil Sticks are said to have traveled from the Middle East to China along the Silk Road. They're still popular with jugglers today. Using two "hand" sticks, the juggler keeps a colorful "flying stick" flipping back and forth through the air.

1 Take the scissors and cut through the first tube on either side of the valve. Do the same with a second tube. Lay the tubes out straight. Cut each tube open along one of the seams to make a long, flat strips of rubber.

2 Cover the ends of the dowels with tape. The shorter dowels are the hand sticks. Use tape to attach one end of a rubber strip onto one of the hand sticks at an angle. Wrap the strip around the stick, overlapping slightly so a ridge spirals up the stick. Secure the other end with tape. Wrap some more tape around the ends to make it look neat. Do the other hand stick the same way.

3 For the flying stick, attach the rubber strip so it is straight, not at an angle. Wrap the rubber three or four times around the end. Then angle the strip and wrap the same way as the hand sticks. When you reach the end, use a small piece of tape to attach the rubber strip to the dowel. Then straighten out the strip and wrap it around the same as at the start. Secure with tape.

4 Cut two rectangular bands of felt, 5 inches (12 centimeters) wide by 6 inches (15 centimeters) long. To make tassels, make cuts about 3 inches (7.5 centimeters) long every ½ inch (1 centimeter) along one of the long edges of each band.

5 Attach the bottom of one tassel band to one end of the flying stick so tassels hang off the end of the stick. Wrap the band around the stick and secure with more tape. Wrap rows of tape tightly around the bottom of the band to hold it in place. Do the same with the other end.

6 Find the center of gravity of the flying stick by balancing it across your thumb. Mark with a ring of tape.

7 To learn how to use the devil sticks, kneel down on the floor or stand in front of a couch. Hold your hands out in front of you, elbows bent, palms facing each other. Stand the flying stick upright between them, with one end on the floor or couch. Let it rest on one hand at a tilt.

8 Begin tapping the flying stick back and forth between your hands, moving them up and down, not side-to-side. This move is called a tick-tock.

9 Next start lifting the flying stick off the floor or couch. Keep practicing until you can keep the tick-tock move going with the flying stick in the air.

10 Now add one stick. Hold the stick a little way in from the end, straight out in front of you. Your first finger should be straight along the stick to keep it steady. When you get the hang of using one stick, add the second.

chapter 7

The Silk Road Today

When the Silk Road was at its height, its cities were full of people from foreign lands, and nomads roamed the steppe on their horses.

Today, things are very different. Some towns still have markets and bazaars with local and handmade goods, but many markets are being replaced by stores with factory-made items. Nomads still live in movable yurts on the plains. But most now spend at least part of the year leading settled lives in the city.

Cities have grown as nomads have settled down. But more people, and more development, have hurt the local environment. Even places that survived the onslaught of the Mongols are now being demolished to make way for new construction. Ancient Silk Road traditions are in danger of being lost.

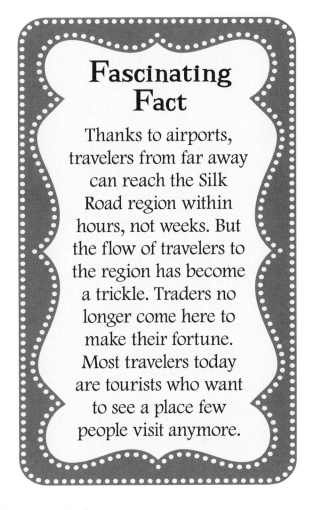

Fascinating Fact

Thanks to airports, travelers from far away can reach the Silk Road region within hours, not weeks. But the flow of travelers to the region has become a trickle. Traders no longer come here to make their fortune. Most travelers today are tourists who want to see a place few people visit anymore.

MAKING SILK ROAD CITIES MODERN

Tashkent in Uzbekistan has more than 3 million people, and is the largest city in Central Asia today. Much of the city had to be rebuilt after a major earthquake in 1966. A few markets and old buildings remain, but for the most part it is a changed city. Many residents would probably say it's a change for the better.

However, in the city of Kashgar in the Xinjiang Uighur Autonomous Region of China, change is not welcomed by all. Kashgar sits high in the Tien Shan Mountains, where the Karakoram Highway from Pakistan meets the old Silk Road.

Until recently, Kashgar held a Sunday market in its Old City that was packed with locals and visitors. In 2009, the Chinese government set out to replace most of the old city center with newer buildings. Families living in houses they had owned for 500 years were moved to apartment buildings on the edge of town. The government claims the new construction is safer in earthquakes, and will bring electricity and other services to the area. But local craftspeople may no longer be able to sell their wares in the central marketplace. The economy may also suffer from the loss of visitors to the former Old City.

ENVIRONMENTAL THREATS TO THE SILK ROAD

Global climate change and growing populations have also become problems in Silk Road cities. For example, bigger farms and factories have been draining water from rivers and wells.

Fascinating Fact

The desert in China has been growing by almost 1,000 square miles a year. As a result, more than 4,000 villages have been abandoned.

The Aral Sea is one of the Silk Road landmarks in trouble. Over the past 30 years, this saltwater lake has shrunk to half its size. Problems started after the former Soviet Union began using the water from freshwater streams that once fed the lake to grow cotton instead.

Today, villages that used to ring the shores of the Aral Sea are gone. Fishing boats rest on the dry sea bottom. The water that's left is too salty for fish, and the entire area has become hotter and drier. Scientists are looking for ways to stop the changes before the lake vanishes altogether.

In the neighboring Hexi Corridor, a more recent problem is massive floods. The area gets its water from the Qilian Mountains on the Tibetan Plateau. But global warming is melting the glaciers on the mountain tops. The glaciers are shrinking at a rate of 23 feet (7 meters) a year, and may be gone entirely by 2050. That means the Hexi Corridor will need to find a new source of water.

CAVES OF A THOUSAND BUDDHAS

Inside the Caves of a Thousand Buddhas near Dunhuang, sand blowing in from the desert has begun to damage wall paintings and statues. Fences and plantings are helping to keep the sand dunes away from the caves. A new visitors center will also help protect the caves from damage caused by the hundreds of thousands of tourists who now come to see the caves each year. ✛

PRESERVING SILK ROAD HISTORY AND CULTURE

Despite the challenges, some groups are working to help keep Silk Road cities alive. One group is the Silk Road Project. It was founded in 1998 by Yo Yo Ma, a Chinese-American musician who is known around the world for his **cello** playing.

The mission of the Silk Road Project is to teach people in the United States and around the world about the Silk Road region through music and the arts. It presents concerts, music recordings, museum exhibits, and other programs. Its performing group, the Silk Road Ensemble, combines old and new music from Eastern and Western traditions.

Another group working to save the Silk Road region is UNESCO, the United Nations Educational, Scientific, and Cultural Organization. UNESCO is dedicated to preserving **World Heritage sites**. Many Silk Road cities are on the World Heritage List. Someday soon, the entire Silk Road route may become a World Heritage site. This may inspire a new generation of visitors to explore the ancient countries of the Silk Road.

words to know

cello: a musical instrument that looks like a large violin.

World Heritage site: places that have historical or cultural importance.

Glossary

abacus: a tool for adding and subtracting using beads on rods.

aksakal: a respected senior member of a tribe, from the Turkic word for "white beard."

alliance: an agreement between two groups to help each other.

altitude: the height of land above the level of the sea.

altitude sickness: a condition that occurs in very high mountains where the air is thin. Too little oxygen in the blood makes a person feel light-headed and nauseous.

archaeologist: a scientist who studies ancient people and their culture by digging ancient sites.

architect: an artist who designs buildings.

arid: dry.

artifact: an ancient, man-made object.

astrolabe: an instrument for finding the position of objects in the sky for navigation.

astrology: an ancient science that tries to use objects in the sky to tell the future.

astronomy: the study of objects in space.

autonomous: self-governing.

Bactrian camel: a two-humped camel native to the Gobi Desert of China.

bamboo: a tree-like type of grass with a hollow woody stem.

barter: to trade by exchanging one kind of good for another.

basin: a bowl-shaped area of rocky ground.

bazaar: a market made up of rows of shops or stalls, sometimes specializing in one thing.

bolt: a roll of fabric.

bronze: a hard, golden metal made by combining copper and tin. Used by early civilizations for tools and weapons.

calligraphy: the art of beautiful writing.

canyon: a deep, narrow valley with steep sides.

caravan: a group of travelers and pack animals on a journey.

caravanserai: an inn providing services and shelter for caravans.

celestial: heavenly.

cello: a musical instrument that looks like a large violin.

Glossary

census: an official count of people living in an area.

civilizations: communities of people that are advanced in art, science, and politics.

clan: groups of families that are related.

cocoon: protective covering made by an insect larva.

commodity: a product made, grown, or gathered for sale.

contagious: easy to catch.

convert: to convince someone to join a new religion.

corridor: a narrow pathway through land that is hard to cross.

Crusades: a series of attacks by European Christians on Muslim rulers over control of the Middle East. The Crusades took place between 1095 and about 1291 CE.

culture: the beliefs and way of life of a group of people.

diplomat: someone who represents a country.

domesticated: bred to be easier for humans to take care of.

dromedary camel: a one-humped camel native to North Africa and Southern Asia.

dynasty: a powerful family or group that rules for many years.

elixir: a liquid with magical properties.

embroidery: the art of making pictures or designs using threads sewn onto fabric.

emperor: the ruler of an empire.

empire: a large group of states and people ruled by a king, called an emperor, or a small group of people.

ethnic group: people with common ancestors sharing customs, languages, and beliefs.

Eurasian Steppe: a large, flat grassland with no trees that stretches across a cool, dry region of Europe and Asia.

exotic: different and exciting.

falconry: using trained falcons to hunt other small birds.

filament: a single thin thread.

geometric: a style of art that uses simple shapes such as lines, circles, and squares.

glacier: a large river of ice that moves down a mountain slope.

glassblowing: making glass bowls or bottles by blowing into a lump of hot, soft glass through a long metal tube.

Glossary

glaze: a glassy coating that waterproofs and decorates pottery.

hajj: a religious trip to Islam's holy sites.

halo: a circle of light around the head of a holy figure.

heretic: a person who disagrees with the traditional beliefs of a religion.

improvise: to make up a piece of music while playing it.

incantation: a magic spell.

incense: a material that is burned to produce a pleasant smell.

irrigation: a system for bringing water through ditches to farmland.

jade: a hard, shiny stone that is usually green. Used for jewelry and sculpture.

Jew: a person who is Jewish, who practices Judaism.

larva: the worm form of an insect.

legend: a story about a hero.

luxury: something expensive. It is not really needed, but it brings pleasure.

madrassa: a Muslim religious school or college.

merchant: someone who buys and sells goods for profit.

metropolis: an important city.

Middle Ages: a period of time from about 350 CE to 1450 CE.

minaret: a high tower used to call Muslims to prayer five times a day.

minerals: naturally occurring solids that have a crystal structure. Gold and diamonds are precious minerals. Rocks are made of minerals.

missionary: someone who tries to win others to his or her faith.

molten: made liquid by heat.

monk: a man who lives in a religious community and devotes himself to prayer.

moral: a valuable lesson to help people know how to behave.

mosque: a Muslim house of worship.

motif: an idea, pattern, image, or theme that is used in many works of art.

mountain pass: a lower place between two mountains where it is easier to cross.

mule: an animal that is a cross between a horse and a donkey.

mummy: a body that has been preserved so that it doesn't decay.

Muslim: a person of the Islamic faith.

Glossary

mutton: meat from an older sheep.

navigation: finding directions for traveling using stars, maps, landmarks, or other methods.

nomads: people who move their homes along regular routes according to the seasons so their animals can find grass and other plants to eat.

oasis: a green area with water in a dry region or desert. The plural of oasis is oases.

oxygen: a gas in the air that animals need to breathe to stay alive.

pagoda: a Buddhist temple, or place of worship, with an upward curving roof.

paiza: a pass for official travelers used in China under Mongol rule.

papyrus: writing material made from strips of the papyrus plant.

parasite: a small insect or other living thing that infects a larger animal and lives off it.

parchment: writing material made from specially prepared animal skin.

pilgrimage: a journey to a place that is important to a religion.

plague: a highly contagious and deadly disease.

plateau: a large, raised area of the earth.

polo: a team game played on horseback by hitting a ball with a long-handled mallet.

porcelain: a type of white pottery that is thin, smooth, and shiny.

preserve: make food last longer.

printing press: a machine that presses inked type onto paper.

profit: the extra money or goods kept after paying costs of doing business.

prophecy: telling the future.

prophet: a person who claims to speak for God.

pseudoscience: false science.

Quran: holy book of Islam.

refuge: a place that gives protection.

religion: a set of beliefs about reality and a god or gods.

Roman Empire: the nation that ruled much of Europe, Africa, and Asia around the Mediterranean Sea from about 753 BCE to about 476 CE.

roof boss: a carved knob that covers where ribs on a ceiling come together.

sacred: a place or object that is worshipped.

Glossary

saddle: a seat for the rider of a horse.

saffron: a cooking spice.

scholar: a person who is highly educated in a subject.

scribe: a person who copies writings by hand.

scroll: a roll of paper or other material containing writing.

sect: a group within a religion whose beliefs are different from that of the main group.

sericulture: the process of making silk.

shagai: an early form of playing dice made from the bones of a sheep.

Silk Road: the ancient network of trade routes connecting the Mediterranean Sea and China by land.

silk: a delicate and beautiful fabric made from the cocoon of a silkworm.

skewer: a thin pointed stick for holding small pieces of food over a fire.

Spice Route: a route by sea from the Spice Islands of Southeast Asia to India, Africa, and Europe.

stirrup: a footrest shaped like a loop used for horseback riding.

sutra: a teaching of Buddha making up part of Buddhist holy writings.

synagogue: a Jewish house of worship.

tax: money charged by a government.

tin: a soft, silvery metal.

trade route: a route used mostly to carry goods from one place to be sold in another.

turban: a long piece of fabric wrapped around the head that completely covers the hair.

World Heritage site: places that have historical or cultural importance.

yak: a large, longhaired ox with curved horns that is native to Tibet.

zodiac: sets of stars in the sky used for astrology.

Resources

BOOKS

Belliveau, Denis and Francis O'Donnell. *In the Footsteps of Marco Polo: A Companion to the Public Television Film.* Rowman & Littlefield Publishers, 2008.

Bonavia, Judy. *The Silk Road: From Xi'an to Kashgar.* Airphoto International, 2004.

Demi, *Marco Polo.* Marshall Cavendish, 2008.

Franck, Irene M. and David Brownstone. *Across Asia by Land.* Facts on File, 1991.

Franck, Irene M. *The Silk Road: A History.* Facts On File, 1988.

Freedman, Russell. *The Adventures of Marco Polo.* Arthur A. Levine Books, 2006.

Gilchrist, Cherry. *Stories from the Silk Road.* Barefoot Books, 2005.

Herbert, Janis. *Marco Polo for Kids: His Marvelous Journey to China, 21 Activities.* Chicago Review Press, 2001.

Kallen, Stuart. *The Working Life - A Medieval Merchant.* Lucent Books, 2005.

Krebs, Laurie. *We're Riding on a Caravan.* Barefoot Books, 2007.

Mack, Rosamond E. *Bazaar to Piazza: Islamic Trade and Italian Art, 1300–1600.* University of California Press, 2001.

Mayhew, Bradley, Paul Clammer and Michael Kohn. *Central Asia.* Lonely Planet Publications, 2004.

Major, John S. and Betty J. Belanus. *Caravan to America: Living Arts of the Silk Road.* Cricket Books, 2002.

Major, John S. *The Silk Route: 7,000 Miles of History.* HarperCollins, 1996.

Polo, Marco. *The Travels.* Translated by Ronald Latham. Penguin Classics, 1958.

Reid, Struan. *Inventions and Trade.* Thameside Press, 2002.

Strathern, Paul. *Exploration by Land.* Thameside Press, 2002.

Ten Grotenhius, Elizabeth (editor). *Along the Silk Road.* Smithsonian Institute, 2002.

Visson, Lynn. *The Art of Uzbek Cooking.* Hippocrene Books, 1998.

WEB SITES

The Silk Road Foundation
www.silkroadfoundation.org

Silk Road Seattle
http://depts.washington.edu/silkroad

Columbia University
The Mongols in World History
http://afe.easia.columbia.edu/mongols

British Library Silk Road Online Gallery
www.bl.uk/onlinegallery/features/silkroad/main.html#

Asia Society, *www.asiasociety.org*

The Silk Road Project, *www.silkroadproject.org*

In the Footsteps of Marco Polo Online Video
www.wliw.org/marcopolo

National Gallery of Art—Artistic Exchange: Europe and the Islamic World
www.nga.gov/exhibitions/2004/artexchange/artexchange_ss.shtm
www.nga.gov/education/classroom/pdf/islamic-tp.pdf

The Three Hares, www.threehares.net

Saudi Aramco World
www.saudiaramcoworld.com

Tea and Carpets, *http://tea-and-carpets.blogspot.com*

Index

Index